R. P. BLACKMUR

ROBERT BOYERS

R. P. BLACKMUR: POET-CRITIC

TOWARD A VIEW OF POETIC OBJECTS

A LITERARY FRONTIERS EDITION

UNIVERSITY OF MISSOURI PRESS

COLUMBIA & LONDON, 1980

Copyright © 1980 by
The Curators of the University of Missouri
University of Missouri Press, Columbia, Missouri 65211
Library of Congress Catalog Card Number 80–15414
Printed and bound in the United States of America

Library of Congress Cataloging in Publication Data

Boyers, Robert.
    R.P. Blackmur, Poet-Critic.

    (A Literary frontiers edition)
    Includes bibliographical references.
    1. Blackmur, Richard P., 1904–1965—Criticism
and interpretation. I. Title.
PS3503.L266Z59   811'.52   80–15414
ISBN 0–8262–0315–9

    "Cool Tombs," by Carl Sandburg, copyright © 1918 by Holt, Rinehart and Winston, Inc., copyright © renewed 1946 by Carl Sandburg; "Masks of Ezra Pound," "The Method of Marianne Moore," "Notes on E. E. Cummings' Language," and "Unappeasable and Peregrine," all from *Language as Gestures* by R. P. Blackmur, copyright © 1951, 1952 by R. P. Blackmur, copyright © renewed 1979 by Elizabeth Blackmur and Mrs. Helen Van Eck. Reprinted by permission of Harcourt Brace Jovanovich, Inc., and George Allen & Unwin, Ltd.
    "The Second Coming," from *The Collected Poems of William Butler Yeats,* copyright © 1924 by Macmillan Publishing Co., Inc., copyright © renewed 1952 by Bertha Georgie Yeats; "A Deep-Sworn Vow," from *The Collected Poems of William Butler Yeats,* copyright © 1919 by Macmillan Publishing Co., Inc., copyright © renewed 1947 by Bertha Georgie Yeats; "Apparitions," from *The Collected Poems of William Butler Yeats,* copyright © 1940 by Georgie Yeats, copyright © renewed 1968 by Bertha Georgie Yeats, Michael Butler Yeats, and Anne Yeats. Reprinted by permission of Macmillan Publishing Co., Inc., and A. P. Watt Ltd., London. "The Moth-Signal" and "The Walk," from *The Collected Poems of Thomas Hardy,* copyright © 1953 by Macmillan Publishing Co., Inc. Reprinted by permission of Macmillan Publishing Co., Inc., and Macmillan Press Ltd., Hampshire.

Research on this study, as on previous studies, was made possible by Skidmore College Faculty Research grants administered by Prof. Eric Weller, Dean of Faculty. My thanks to Professor Weller.

The Double Agent (essays), 1935
From Jordan's Delight (verse), 1937
The Expense of Greatness (essays), 1940
The Second World (verse), 1942
The Good European (verse), 1947
Language as Gesture (essays), 1952: This volume contains most of the essays on poets and poetry that Blackmur wished to preserve, including pieces on Dickinson, Hardy, Yeats (2), Pound (2), Eliot (2), Stevens (3), Moore, Lawrence, Crane, and Cummings. Also there are several book reviews and position papers on the practice of criticism.

The Lion and the Honeycomb (essays), 1955: This volume includes critical essays on Henry Adams, Henry James, Herman Melville, Irving Babbitt, T. E. Lawrence. It also contains studies of the critical process and of general cultural issues ("The Politics of Human Power," "The Artist as Hero," and so on).

Anni Mirabiles, 1921-1925: Reason in the Madness of Letters (four Library of Congress lectures), 1956

Eleven Essays in the European Novel, 1964: This volume contains studies of Dostoevski, Flaubert, Tolstoy, Mann, and Joyce.

A Primer of Ignorance (essays), 1967: This is a posthumous collection edited by Joseph Frank, including miscellaneous papers on ballet, Toynbee, travel, Henry Adams; also, the *Anni Mirabiles* lectures.

Henry Adams, 1980: An unfinished work, written mostly in the 1940s and 1950s, with several sections published in earlier collections. Edited by Veronica Makowsky.

I. INTRODUCTION: POET-CRITIC

 F ifty years ago, when R. P. Blackmur published his first essays on the poetry of his time, he could assume that people with literary interests read poems. He could believe that critics were among those readers, and that they were disposed to assist others in the proper reception and analysis, even in the judgment and appreciation, of new works. There were jobs to be done, services to be provided, and one did not need to be modest to remember that—with few exceptions—"there are no statues to critics and scholars" and that, after "putting the audience into relation to the work of art," those grey figures are usually content to disappear.

At present, the critics at least have decided not to disappear. They have decided that there are better things to do than to play the role of shoehorn—Pound's image—to someone else's shoe. This means, in effect, that critics now demand for their activity a recognition that is in no way subordinate to the recognition typically accorded the "creative" activity of painters, novelists, and poets. Nor is this an issue that may be argued in a sustained or fruitful way. Criticism is or is not a fundamental and life-enhancing activity: who will settle the question to the satisfaction of all parties? What is clear, however, is that—partly as a consequence of changes in the status of criticism—poetry in our time has ceased to command interest even in the degree that it did fifty years ago. Then at least literary people argued over *The Waste Land*. And those who were capable of working themselves up over Eliot's literary essays would surely have been willing to read the relevant pages in Milton and Shelley so as to make up their minds about the issues Eliot raised.

No more. Literary academics—with few exceptions— read only critical and scholarly books. They argue theories and methodologies. For pleasure some take up an occasional novel. Books of poetry, even when they are competently distributed by major publishers, go begging. Critics know that, when they bother to write about the poetry of their time, they will be writing in the main for half-literate

1

students with assignments to complete. And with this fact in view, any essay that keeps its eye on the poem-text will be dismissed by most literary professionals as "practical criticism" growing out of an absurdly modest sense of the critic's calling. To serve the poem or to seek to bridge the gap between poet and reader is, after all, to assume that there is a special value in the poem, that it does something that cannot be done so well in another way. And this precisely most literate people today will not accept; or, if they do accept the proposition, they do so not because they have a lively interest in poems but because they have a professional stake in positioning themselves on one side or another of literary propositions. Poetry is not just another "minority" art like ballet and modern music. Increasingly, it is an art for practitioners only. Even the practitioners find that they can afford to interest themselves only in the poetry they can use, that they can summon nothing like a disinterested concern for the progress of forms. Poetry has few readers, while the critics speak endlessly of poetic renovation and the poets generate volume after volume that no one will read.

Now it is up to the publishers, and poets, to lament the fact that few people today buy poetry, that even those who teach poetry in the university will own no more than the volumes they need to teach from. But it is a fact that, if the popularity of poetry is declining in our culture, the decline has much to do with the erosion not merely of valuable disciplines but of habits of thought we shall be hard put to recover. And that is a fact that ought to interest those in the laity who yet have it in them to worry over such things.

Those who worry—whether poets, critics, or laity— will know better than to blame critics or criticism exclusively for what has come to pass. They will know also that more than improvements in literary criticism will be required to bring to mind essential changes. But we have in contemporary criticism an indication of what has gone wrong. And we have, in the early writings of R. P. Blackmur especially, a model of right thinking that might serve as a corrective to more recent theory and practice. What has gone wrong? Briefly, and limiting ourselves to recent developments in literary analysis, we might offer the following: Criticism in our time is disfigured by two related, though really quite distinct, tendencies. Many critics write as if poems existed

2

for the sake of theoretical structures that may be said to precede or to underlie the poems themselves. They aim to move away from poems, which are described as contingent structures too often bent on containing rather than releasing essential truths, toward an autonomous poetics that can be manipulated only by cadres of trained theorists.

The second tendency mistakes poems for a content identified with detachable ideas that are acceptable—or not—in the degree in which they conform to current views on human being, sex roles, political virtue, and so on. Practitioners of this criticism stand as far away from poems as do those who subscribe to the other tendency. But they are after different things. The first group includes people who may once have had a genuine interest in actual poems but have become too sophisticated to concern themselves with local effects. The critic Joseph N. Riddel, in his recent book on William Carlos Williams,[1] speaks for his colleagues in the "movement" when he announces that poetics is the subject of the modern and postmodern poem. The great poets themselves, apparently, would have become theorists if only they had the talent. For it is clear to Riddel and to other influential followers of Jacques Derrida that the critic can come closer to realizing what are after all the goals of poets as well.

This we may not say of critics in the second group, much though many of them have been tempted by the continental preenings of their more glamorous colleagues. The more modest critics continue to think of themselves as serving poetry in their commitment to ideas and to rigorous procedures by which one notion may be distinguished from another. They think of themselves as waging a rear-guard action against others in the profession who refuse to believe that poetry can speak to us. Their object is to locate what is relevant in contemporary poems and to establish an acceptable perspective from which we will be encouraged to take seriously the poetry of our time. The operant assumption is that poems attach us to particular habits of thought or to great ideas by talking about them. By getting at those habits or ideas, by collecting usable insights from the poems, the critic is thought to enlighten the reader and, not inciden-

1. Joseph N. Riddel, *The Inverted Bell* (Baton Rouge: Louisiana State University Press, 1974).

tally, to make it possible for him to go back to the poems equipped to extract the central insights for himself. Even so accomplished a critic as J. Hillis Miller—lately identified as a member of the first group—may be said to have contributed to this tendency by reading poems as if they were statements about subjects the poet addresses equally well in essays and other less formal communications. Miller's classic study, *Poets of Reality*,[2] may stand as a particularly inspired example of the tendency we have meant to describe, collecting a line from this poem, three from that, along with a passage from a letter or essay, all with a view toward underlining some view the reader would do well to consider. In this, no one is to wonder why the "evidence" may as well be taken from an undistinguished fragment as from the central stanza of a major poem. The assumption is, if the poet said it, he must have meant it, and the business of the critic is to construct from what he has found the essential pattern. That this will necessarily be the pattern not of a poetic enquiry but of a finished thought should not seem to anyone to compromise what most of us have always taken the poem to be.

Though Richard Palmer Blackmur came in his later years to think himself a theorist, he would not have agreed that poetics is the exclusive subject of the modern poem. And though he became progressively attached to particular ideas—chiefly literary ideas—he never mistook them for *the things themselves:* for the poems and novels he wished to celebrate and analyze. He was attracted to systems and structures but was ever sensible of the human losses entailed in too thorough an absorption in abstraction. Always ready to discourse, he cultivated from the first an acute sense of all the important things even his own adaptable discourses could not get at. And he knew that, if it was the business of poems to intimate what could not be said in any other way, it was the business of criticism to foster a respect for limits and an anticipation of the experience the poem alone could furnish.

Blackmur was, for most of his career, identified with the New Criticism. In his earliest books—in my view, his best books—he was attentive to poetic detail very much in

2. J. Hillis Miller, *Poets of Reality* (Cambridge, Mass.: Harvard University Press, 1965).

the degree we associate with other writers like William Empson and Cleanth Brooks. He did surely subscribe to Brooks's view of the poem as "a simulacrum of reality— . . . an experience rather than any mere statement about experience or any mere abstraction from experience." But he was not, like Empson, impatient with mystery, irritated by the inexplicable. He would not have boasted, in the words of Stanley Edgar Hyman, "of having converted something 'magical' through analysis into something 'sensible,' " though like Empson that is what he sometimes did.[3] In fact, though Blackmur believed in approaching literature through technique, he never thought technique sufficient, either for poets or critics. He was much closer than other New Critics to Eliot's view that, in poetry as in criticism, "the only method is to be very intelligent." Blackmur was a New Critic in his commitment to texts and to the particular words of texts. He was not a mechanical interpreter with eyes only for meanings he might carry away like so many trophies.

The New Critics, of course, are no longer honored as once they were. Their belief in the primacy of poetry itself seems no longer supportable, and what were once thought practical defects are now thought to be larger deficiencies of attitude and vision. For some people, scrupulous attention to the technical dynamics, even to the diction of a poem must be regarded as an arid, self-perpetuating formula, a reflection of scrupulosity, not intelligence. Others regard the New Critics simply as political reactionaries, mystifying the reader's relation to texts by installing between them an elaborate methodological apparatus and insisting that truth is nothing more than the truth of a particular poem. Those who cannot bring themselves to condescend to the New Critics may praise them for "strong" readings of texts, for their willingness to make poems say what the critics themselves want them to say. This support, in terms of which creative misreading is indistinguishable from correct interpretation and evaluation, amounts to a rejection of everything people like Brooks and Blackmur thought they were about.

3. See Stanley Edgar Hyman's *The Armed Vision* (New York: Alfred A. Knopf, 1947) for extended treatments of Blackmur, Empson, and other "modern" critics.

But it was not for more recent critics alone to question the value of New Criticism. Even at the height of its influence there were questions, and many were posed by writers who had every reason to be pleased with the labors of the New Critics. The poet Delmore Schwartz, in an essay originally published in 1938,[4] spoke of "the serious abstraction, incompleteness, and omission involved in Blackmur's whole method" and complained that "the vast machinery brought forward" was often excessive. While applauding Blackmur as by far the most useful and illuminating of critics, and hoping that his "method" would continue to spread, he warned against the abuses of New Criticism and worried over its tendency to keep form and content apart. Even worse was its inclination to assume that substance was an insignificant part of the experience of a poem. "In his analysis of *Sunday Morning*," Schwartz writes, "Blackmur gives us just so much about Stevens' substance as will justify and elucidate Stevens' use of certain words and images." This is a damning observation, to be sure. But it has more to do with the practice of other New Critics than with Blackmur, and anyone who has read the famous essays on Stevens will know that Schwartz was badly mistaken.

We shall have occasion in this study to consider in some detail Schwartz's cautionary strictures, but it is important here to note that they had an extraordinary and unfortunate impact on Blackmur. In the early essays on Stevens, Cummings, Pound, and others, Blackmur had seemed to know exactly what he was after. He could indicate, with no intention of apology, that he meant here to follow up these observations, there to pursue something else entirely. His forays were at once authoritative and provisional. The critic would allow himself to be guided by the work and by his own visceral responses to examine what seemed to him essential. He conceded gladly that his procedures were more suited to discovering these things than those and often suggested alternative ways of going about the critic's business. He was as easy bringing to bear a scholarly reference as he was relying on a hunch. In time, though,

4. See "The Critical Method of R. P. Blackmur," in *Selected Essays of Delmore Schwartz*, ed. Donald A. Dike and David H. Zucker (Chicago: University of Chicago Press, 1970).

Blackmur grew apologetic. One wishes he had instead grown arrogant and defensive. In the late forties he began to write those essays on the function of criticism at the present time that so often confuse and dismay students of a significant body of critical work. For the position papers frequently have nothing useful to say about what it is the critic really does when he examines a work of art. They pretend to describe a procedure and to rule out certain excesses, but they usually respond to the climate of literary opinion by striking empty postures and throwing hostile readers off the critic's trail. "The Lion and the Honeycomb" (1950) and "A Burden for Critics" (1948) are just such performances. Without in so many words holding himself guilty as charged by Schwartz and others, Blackmur indicts the tendency of New Criticism to become an empty methodology: "I fear," he writes, "that if new growth is not undertaken there may be only a false and sterile life." The New Critics—and it is clear he speaks here of himself as of John Crowe Ransom and Brooks and the others—have relied upon their considerable linguistic skills as if these were adequate for all of the critical tasks to be performed. What they gave us is a combination of "excess analysis, excess simplification, and excess application."

Blackmur's repudiation of excess in his own critical procedure might be thought to mark a refreshing self-knowledge and self-correction. Nothing could be further from the facts. Blackmur's essays on British and American modernist poetry are marked by neither excess analysis nor excess simplification. They seem to a number of us to include the best analyses of Hardy, Moore, Cummings, Crane, and Lawrence that have yet been written. Others among them—like the essays on Yeats and Pound—are dated in the sense that it is possible now to say essential things about those poets that Blackmur could not possibly have known when he wrote his essays. But as essays they too are impressively rich and useful works that contemporary critics still refer to. In short, for whatever reasons, Blackmur came to believe that he too had better things to do than to write the best essays on poets and poetry that anyone had ever written. He bought the notion that an ambitious critic was well advised to move away from texts, to discover Ideas, to talk about things instead of allowing his discourses to be penetrated by the voice and thought

7

rhythms of poets and their verses. He pretends, in his position papers, to be as attached as ever to "technical judgment" and to be interested still in "recreating . . . a verbal sensibility capable of coping with the poetry." But he ceased effectively to write about poetry by the late forties, and much that he wrote in the period between 1950 and his death in 1965 is simply unreadable.

There are those who feel that Blackmur got better and better the further he removed himself from texts and responded to ideas. Joseph Frank, for example, suggests that what was wanted was the "widening of scope and approach" that we find in the later works.[5] It is true, Frank agrees, that Blackmur moved, in his essays on the novel and on thinkers like Henry Adams, "in the direction of an analogical affability that dissolves all formal, historical, and cultural boundaries in the warmth of its embrace." But in place of the "specific insight" and the "finer and finer discriminations" readers came to expect of him, Blackmur is said to have provided "the revelatory citation," "criticism by aphoristic assertion rather than by explanation." We may not be able to make out half of what he says, and no one would be so foolish as to apply the insights thrown off like so many sparks from the critic's blazing workroom. Blackmur founded no schools, established no firm precedents, and inspired few general readers. No matter. He got away from those New Critical exercises and confronted the world without a repertoire of artificial techniques to protect him. Even Frank, who understood clearly Blackmur's growing inclination to provide "more a shot in the dark than a definition," continued to feel that his old friend and teacher was well advised to abandon his earlier procedures. The critic Donald Davie may have gone too far in proposing that in his later efforts "Mr. Blackmur seems to have gone off the rails," but there is no doubt in my mind that he misconceived entirely the nature of his gift and, consequently, of his peculiar mission.

Blackmur was a poet. He published in his lifetime three volumes of verse and hoped that some of his work at least would stand. At present he has almost no readers. At a time

5. See "R. P. Blackmur: The Later Phase," in Joseph Frank's volume, *The Widening Gyre* (New Brunswick: Rutgers University Press, 1963).

when so little poetry is read, it is not surprising that a small voice like Blackmur's should not be heard. Some critics, like Denis Donoghue, in an introduction to a recent collected edition of the poems,[6] regret that we have forgotten Blackmur and urge us to discover the poetry for ourselves. But Donoghue is a fine critic, and even he cannot persuade us that there is much in Blackmur to compel sustained attention. "Sometimes the knowledge in Blackmur's poems is not his own but what he recalls of Hopkins' knowledge," he concedes. Or one hears the music of Eliot, or Pound, or Yeats: "But mostly the knowledge is his own." Perhaps. But then, the issue is not whether Blackmur occasionally broke free of his models and wrote in a voice that sounded more like his own than theirs. The fact is that, even in his best poems, Blackmur sounds more like a man who wants to write poetry than like a true poet. Donoghue does well to point out the poet's strengths and goes so far as to name his best poems. Mostly he talks around the poems and discusses Blackmur's view of poetry. The stress is, unavoidably, on Blackmur's great work as a critic of the modernist masters he so wished to emulate and join. Blackmur's biographer, Russell Fraser,[7] reminds us that J. V. Cunningham and Yvor Winters thought him a most engaging and brilliant poet. Then one remembers how poorly other judgments of these critics have worn.

Robert Lowell, who thought Blackmur "a good poet, weird, tortured, derivative, original," was closer to the mark in declaring him "more a poet in his criticism." The observation places Blackmur precisely and introduces a view of the man that differentiates him from the other New Critics with whom he was too often confused. Empson, of course, was a fine poet, but it was not the voice—nor even the characteristic concerns—of the poet one heard in his criticism. The poet and the critic were more distinct in him than in Blackmur. And this was true as well of Tate and of Ransom. Nor would one think to speak of Eliot as a "poet-critic." He was the one, and he was the other. But there are writers, like Blackmur, of whom it is possible to say that

6. *Poems of R. P. Blackmur* (New Jersey: Princeton University Press, 1977).
7. See the excerpt from Russell Fraser's biography-in-progress in the *Sewanee Review* 87:3 (Summer 1979).

they bring to their main business—criticism—the concerns and the sensibility of the poet. The term *poet-critic* is not always used with so careful a sense of what in fact it designates, but there is good reason to apply it now with greater care. Lowell used the term frequently to describe writers he admired. Randall Jarrell, in his view, was a poet-critic; so was Donald Davie, whose "prose rings." Shortly before his death, Lowell extended the designation to Robert Pinsky, who "belongs to that rarest category of talents, a poet-critic."[8] Now it is not clear in any of these cases that Lowell thought less of the writer's verse than of his prose. Surely he was an avid backer of Jarrell's poetry, though he might secretly have supported the popular view that Jarrell gave his genius to his criticism, leaving only the talent for the verse.

In any case, Lowell helped to circulate a designation that will appear to have a special aptness for Blackmur. Like Jarrell, he achieved with his criticism—for a time at least—a remarkable impact. Readers took him to speak with the authority of a man who had devoted himself to poetry, who was alert to the kinds of particulars none but practicing poets would care about. The authority did not derive from his stature as a great poet who had a claim to be the presiding voice or spirit of his age. This might have been true in some sense of Eliot, but could never have been true of Jarrell or Blackmur. Blackmur's authority derived from the fact that he sounded like a man whose thought had been in part taken over by the poets he studied. He thought like a poet, not in his poetry, but in his criticism. It wasn't that he indulged flights of patently poetic rhetoric or opted for vagueness when he might have aimed at precision. He was a poet-critic in the sense that he knew what devices poets used to generate effects and, frequently, to make their art do for them what they couldn't manage in their thought; and he knew exactly how a reader might be assisted to understand a poem by learning to put himself provisionally in the place of one who thinks poetically. He could speak of the

8. Lowell's comments appear as solicited statements on the dust jackets of books by Davie and Pinsky. His remarks on Jarrell may be found in *Randall Jarrell, 1914-1965*, ed. R. Lowell, P. Taylor, R. P. Warren (New York: Farrar, Straus & Giroux, 1967).

10

poet's deception not at first with a view toward impugning it but with the intention of discovering what the reader would have to do to acquiesce in it in good faith and with no betrayal of intelligence. Here was a criticism that demonstrated, in every sentence, that the poet has his reasons, and that a properly disinterested intelligence will not need to forfeit its own procedures to submit to what in the poetry has a legitimate claim on our sympathies.

As the great poet-critic of the modernist period— Jarrell's criticism already seems soft and easy to settle into by contrast—Blackmur proved that it was possible to establish a strong critical voice without in any sense challenging the priority of the poets and their work. He could not have anticipated the way in which criticism in our time has taken the place of poetry as an object of reverent attention, but he was surely aware of relevant problems. The main problem, as he saw it, was that close readers of poems would become so attached to their techniques and to their own exegetical versions that they would cease to be readers in the proper sense. He overreacted to Schwartz and to others who were skeptical of New Criticism, but he was quite right to fear that the elaboration of literary doctrine might soon seem more important to critics than the full activity of response. The discipline of reading was itself at issue. So versatile and original a literary mind as Kenneth Burke's exhibited the tendency Blackmur feared in the hands of less distinguished critics. Burke was far from a New Critic and rarely cared to provide "an account of literature"; he did take poetry as an object of attention and was routinely disposed to treat it as a matter "subordinate to rhetoric in the beginning and in the end to be transformed into rhetoric." Burke was an example of the literary mind pursuing its own doctrines and systems—sometimes brilliantly, sometimes in infuriating disregard of alternative options. To submit to his spell was to be engulfed, to feel that for such a critic there is

> no need to stop and there is nothing to arrest him: there are no obstacles he cannot transform into abstract or reduce to neutral terms in his rhetoric. He is a very superior example indeed of the mind in which the articulate organization has absorbed the material organized . . . The methodology is a wonderful machine that creates its own image out of

everything fed into it. Nobody means what he says but only the contribution of what he says to the methodology.[9]

Blackmur was a little uneasy about using Burke in this way, as a symptom of a condition that might have been better diagnosed in others. But the challenge to emergent academic and theoretical orthodoxies was posed in a vivid and plausible critique that might well be used to address contemporary excesses that come under the heading of "The Anxiety of Influence" or "Structuralist Poetics." Blackmur was not concerned about the triumph of one critical school over another; he wanted to preserve the habit of literary response that he took to be a fundamental model of the mind working properly. The critic who found "nothing to arrest him" had managed to dispense with the intransigeant otherness of objects. Such objects were required to compel the mind to instruct itself in the arts of negotiation. Response was, for Blackmur, a process of submission and aggression, a wary taking in and a tentative recasting of the given materials. Those materials were never to be greedily "absorbed" or definitively transformed. They were to be respected and preserved in their otherness even as they were worked upon by the critic's re-creative techniques. Blackmur resorted more than once in his writings to the term *dialectical* to describe what he particularly valued in the operations of mind. Criticism was to be an account of the mind conversing with itself, working out its relations with that which was separate and was given to make compelling demands of its own. Poetry was not of reality but of experience, and experience could be met only with the responsive questions of one who imagined himself also capable of experience. One of Blackmur's best critics, Richard Foster, described him as "a poet *creating* consciousness, *creating* in his readers a preparatory semblance of the essential experience to come in the poem proper."[10] There is more to say about this, but for the moment it will have to do as a valid description of Blackmur's exemplary critical activity. He was no interpreter-drudge. He managed at once to do a job of

9. See the title essay of Blackmur's collection *The Lion and the Honeycomb* (New York: Harcourt, Brace and Co., 1955).
10. Blackmur figures prominently in Richard Foster's *The New Romantics* (Bloomington: Indiana University Press, 1962).

work, to shoulder a specific tutelary burden, and to further the progress of consciousness.

In this study, then, I shall dwell upon Blackmur's work as a poet-critic. I take this work to be an essential corrective to much that passes for critical discourse in our time. And I believe, also, that the decline of poetry in our time can be halted and reversed only by the recovery of modes of poetical thinking exhibited in Blackmur's early essays. I shall stress in my study the dimension of "rational imagination" so often underscored by Blackmur and either scorned or ignored by many prominent critics nowadays. By this I shall mean nothing so narrow or mean spirited as the concept may once have seemed in the writings of Winters or, here and there, in the more curmudgeonly performances of F. R. Leavis. With "rational imagination" in view, I shall refer only for emphasis or contrast to Blackmur's later writings on the art of fiction or Ideas in History. The reader who feels there is better use to be made of the later criticism will be looking for a book—short or long—that is very different from mine. So, too, will the reader who believes that a defensible case may be made for the centrality of Blackmur's own verse. Fraser, in the portions of the impending critical biography he has released for periodical publication, shows that he has an appetite for the larger work to be done. Mine is, in every sense, an essay.

II. TOWARD A VIEW OF POETIC OBJECTS

In "The Swan In Zurich," an audacious late essay on the art of dance,[1] Blackmur reflects upon style and technique as expressions of national character. A passionate admirer of George Balanchine's New York City ballet, he wonders why it is that Americans brought up on Balanchine have so little patience for English companies. The question might well be asked today, more than twenty years later. The issue is never settled, but Blackmur suggests it all has something to do with technique. Americans, he contends, characteristically rely upon and glorify technique to the exclusion of substance. The indulgence of story and of sentimental association in English ballet, the reliance upon costume and stage setting, seem to Americans of a certain experience "soft" and "sloppy." English dancers seem not to exhibit "technique" or finish in the sense in which they are admired by American audiences. An American abroad is forced to wonder about the origins of his own predilections and to apply to them some corrective insight. This he can manage to do only by examining the object of his affection with a view toward discerning its essential nature and identifying what it leaves out in order to assume the shape it has.

As in so many of his essays, Blackmur does best when he is least interested in sweeping generalization. In the ballet study, for example, he never really persuades us that the distinctions he draws have much to do with national character. It is plausible to contend that Americans have made a fetish of technique in film or dance, or that "French logic" in the arts is manifested in a resistance to sweetness and a paradoxical slide into "external muddle." But it is equally possible to argue that these are glib observations, and that in any case Blackmur doesn't care enough about them to try them out in other essays. By contrast, his observations on the spirit of a certain kind of American dance are

1. In *A Primer of Ignorance,* ed. Joseph Frank (New York: Harcourt, Brace and World, 1967). The essay was written in 1958.

not susceptible to easy dismissal, and represent not so much a mode of cultural commentary as of textual analysis. Here the text is not a poem but a dance composition, and the critic shows that it is possible to train upon movement in space the kind of attention ordinarily directed toward words on the page. This is instructive, not because it shows off the versatility of Blackmur's critical tools, but because the discriminations he draws in responding to Balanchine's dancers may help us understand what he sometimes says about literary works.

Blackmur doesn't, in presuming to write on American dance, anticipate the objections of dance experts. He fails to say that American dance is not Balanchine alone, but Martha Graham and Merce Cunningham and all of the other figures associated for fifty years and more with the modern-dance movement. All the same, it is fair to say that Balanchine is the great master of dance in this century, and that he has created a central style that affects the way dance is regarded not only in the United States but in every western nation. Blackmur is quite within his rights to focus upon Balanchine. To arrive at his more general cultural observations—which he'd have been well advised to forego —Blackmur identifies technique as the determining factor in Balanchine dance. He might better have said, for technique, impersonality, since everything in his intimate response to the dancing itself indicates that is what he means. He speaks of the creation of "a great beauty" and of "terrifying vision" as if these might conceivably be the achievement of refined technique alone. But he knows better, and only his will to cultural diagnosis and prediction prompts him to insist implausibly upon what can only be an aspect of the dancing he observes. This is not, I would insist, a matter of opinion, though it would be if Blackmur did not so accurately and scrupulously represent the object of his attention: if he did not so sharply communicate the look and feel of the dancers going through their motions. We can see from what Blackmur says of the dance—especially if we have seen and considered the relevant dances for ourselves—that he provides implicitly a critique of the general conclusions he draws. He allows us to identify the points at which particular response gives way to general or ideological response. And he makes us—quite without meaning to do so—

properly suspicious of an ideological response that does not consistently attend to the epiphenomena that constitute its necessary foundation.

Blackmur is reflecting upon Balanchine's *Concerto Barocco,* a dance composition scored to the music of Bach's Double Violin Concerto. He is moved by the precision and purity of the work, a purity that is a function of design and of a "proficiency beyond conceivable impulse." No impurity of personal motive, no ordinary object or message may be said to intrude upon the rigorous working out of the design for its own sake. The critic thinks, almost inevitably, of Ortega's work on the Dehumanization of Art and states: "It was a magnificent technique for expunging the psyche—who is slow and stubborn, and always purposeful with however much uncertainty—from the body which danced." So, too, is psyche, or psychological motive, absent from the experience of the viewer, who is, like Blackmur, "caught up, a fly in invisible eddies." The dance steps are visible enough, but the energy that drives them seems impossible to locate; the ends to which the forms have been assembled seem a trivial irrelevance. Blackmur considers what he calls an "almost 'closed' performance," in which "the subject is left out," in which "a great beauty . . . is devastated of everything but form and gait." The viewer is all rapt, even hysterical attention, "whirled in the moral vortex of art." There is an impression of a terrible beauty, detached from ordinary human referents, abstract in the thoroughness of its self-absorption. The critic who would hold on to purpose—"with however much uncertainty"—is driven to resist "the unscrupulousness of motion so hard it inched on the brittle." Even as he seeks to engage the object, to meet it on its own hard terms, Blackmur is compelled toward a language of moral resistance. The hardness that is a function of studied impersonality and meticulous design seems to him something else, like a willful denial of the prospect of human meeting and concession."What is so hard," Blackmur asks, "as hysteric exactness, unless it be abstract exclusiveness?"

One wonders, of course, why the critic should feel drawn to expect from Balanchine an expression of human vulnerability. Why should cool mastery and easy precision be equated with "hysteric exactness"? "Hysteric" suggests underlying incompatibilities that have been resolutely, even dishonestly, suppressed. The assumption at work is that a certain kind of exactness is compensatory, that it necessarily covers over other kinds of commitments that the artist feels he cannot claim or acknowledge. What those commitments would be in a dance composition that has no narrative element I cannot begin to say, but Blackmur clearly feels that significant loss and suppression are involved. He is not ready to dismiss the *Concerto Barocco* or to deny that it has the power to take hold of him and to move him to wonder. But he does not like what such a response implicitly means, what it makes of him.

But let us consider a little further what Blackmur actually sees—and what he misses—in the dance work. He sees what he takes to be a variety of accomplished performance forms that can be learned by "anyone with intelligence and docility." Again, technique is the central term of derogation, "and it represents what can be repeated from one work to another without regard to substance or gift." What he misses is human presence, even in dancers who may be human all too human in their private comings and goings. In thrall to the dance to which they have given themselves, he argues, "they had no faces and no legs that were inhabited. Some kind of sex was missing here—the tenderness—the predatoriness—the sexuality itself." There is, in place of a wholeness to which viewers might respond with their own wholeness, only a "great initial beauty" eliciting technical or "merely" aesthetic enthusiasms.

It is possible to differ with Blackmur about the impression produced by Balanchine dancers performing the *Concerto Barocco*. It is possible, for example, to argue that the dancers generate a kind of sexuality that usually has nothing to do either with tenderness or predatoriness. One may feel the erotic charge without being able to identify what it is. But that is not for our purposes a useful difference to pursue. Better to grant what Blackmur says about the absence of sexuality, remembering that Balanchine has created dozens of highly charged erotic works that are no less formally intricate than the Bach piece and no less reliant upon built-in expressive constraints. When we grant Blackmur his point, we remember also that the demand for personal presence, for sexual charge in a work of art grows out of other demands that are obviously different. Blackmur objects, for example, to works in which "we decide on our perfections ahead of time." To aim at technical perfections is in this sense to know too well what we are after. "This should, I think"—and here Blackmur rises to a pitch of rejection that would seem to belie his own powerful attraction to Balanchine ballet—"be called whoring before the arts with only half our natural skills and wiles. What is forgotten is that all true techniques draw on the chthonic for their substance— . . . as a gesture comes to birth beyond, and *with*, every skill of nerve and muscle." The critic demands that the work refuse to assign itself determinate goals, that it discover what it can do as it goes about its proper business, which is the business of discovery. What it discovers will not be a particular thought-form or idea but a mode in which particular sensations or ideas may be taken in. Always, in the discovery or generation of modes of apprehension, there is implicit recognition of what may not be encompassed, what may only be gestured at or tried on with an assertion of utter provisionality. This comes, for Blackmur, under the heading of "chaos," and it is quite simply all that "we do not know, or ignore, of the behavior which, in all the versions of space and time we can manage, forms our lives." It seems to me a mistake to speak in this regard of "behavior," but Blackmur is quite legitimately concerned about the reach of dance as an art form in a way that should recommend itself to practitioners of other forms as well. If he speaks of the exclusion of chaos from a work of dance, he testifies to an absence he takes to be remediable. Though he is not willing to propose solutions to address this absence, he does identify something that distinguishes the work of art when it is equal to its resources.

So, for Blackmur, the dance composition is required to do what a poem does, despite their obvious differences. If Balanchine relies too heavily upon technique, if his words give the impression of having been made up, of allowing for no genuine discovery on the part of artist, dancer, or spectator, he may be accused of denying himself the full exploration of his own creative possibilities. At the heart of Blackmur's argument is the contention that, for an art form that invests so much in the extensions of the human body, Balanchine dance is curiously deficient in human presence. This presence the critic identifies with sexual aura. It draws its substance from "the chthonic," from the earth itself, which is to say, from the very foundations of a human civilization structured around human needs and capacities. Sexual aura, in dance, is a manifest of the work's continuing contact with its own origins. As an enactment—even of a drama without name or narrative predictability—the dance is required to body forth in some way the aetiological myth from which it takes its implicit direction. *Concerto Barocco,* in its combination of severity and easy grace, ought somehow to carry within it some traces of the pressures with which it contends, of the impulses it has to transform to be what it so gloriously is. Blackmur complains because it seems to him that the work has no wish to acknowledge what it really is. The dancers themselves would no doubt tell him that there is always in dance conflict and resistance; there is quite obviously the force of gravity holding performers to the dance floor when they would rise and move about in perfect disregard of their own weight. That force at least they must, however disdainfully, acknowledge. But Blackmur wants more and concludes that technical finish of a certain kind can elicit only a vulgar enthusiasm. The spectator may hold his breath and exclaim, but he is, apparently, left with very little. Nothing is satisfactorily transformed.

Now it seems to me that Blackmur is really quite wrong about *Concerto Barocco,* and that he does not really understand the spirit of Balanchine dance. For it is not the business of that dance to provide substance of the kind Blackmur seeks. It is a commonplace that the dancers in a Balanchine company give off, frequently, an aura that is more than human—Blackmur might say less than human. And it is a fact that Balanchine has often spoken of his favorite dancers as material upon which he sculpts. One body, one face, may have and make use of expressive capacities not available to another, but in essence all are subject to the disciplines and shapings imposed upon them by their "maker." At their best they express emotions—ranging from erotic excitement (*Stravinsky Violin Concerto*) to sophisticated insouciance (*Who Cares*) and tender submission (the final movement of *The Prodigal Son*)—but those emotions are embodied in so pure a state that they may not be said to remind us directly of our own vulnerabilities. The emotions are refined almost to the point of abstraction. They compel engagement in the sense precisely that they invoke chthonic depths. It is, if you will, only the form of the relevant emotion that they enact. What Blackmur calls

19

"sexuality itself" is provided only where—as one sometimes sees—there is a discrepancy between the forms of the work, its "lines," and their enactment by a dancer whose body seems somehow oddly matched with those lines. This oddness introduces human presence into the work in a way that is peculiar for an art otherwise so chastely and rigorously designed. One sees the oddness, for example, in Balanchine's use of a dancer whose legs are rather longer and fuller than one would expect of the figure asked to wrap her legs around the body of a small man and to climb upward from his knees to his shoulders. Here the chthonic invocation of seduction and compliance takes on a sexual dimension it might otherwise contain without so much as making the spectator aware of it. Some may think the oddness a detriment to the work, while others will approve the consequent "humanizing" of the experience. Blackmur would say that any acceptable element not absolutely programmed into the design and utterly, inflexibly controlled would be all to the good. The tendency to go against the grain of the abstract design would be said to reduce the mechanical reliance on sheer technique and to give an impression of conflict. The dancers would seem somehow really to inhabit those painted faces and practiced bodies that too often threaten to assume the lifeless quality of objects agitated from without.

What Blackmur is less willing to accept in dance than in poetry is the autonomous life of the work itself, the sense in which it proposes its own objects and manages to be, or not to be, adequate to them. He might, for correction, have called to mind the conventions associated with what Frank Kermode calls the "romantic image." In his classic book of that name,[2] Kermode describes what he takes to be central in the poetry of late romanticism, namely, its concentration in images of a strange radiance. These images, in the words of Joyce's Stephen Dedalus, produce a beauty that is "apprehended as one thing . . . self-bounded and self-contained upon the immeasurable background of space or time which is not it." The artist's mind, creating and reflecting all at once, is moreover arrested in a "luminous stasis of esthetic pleasure." It feeds upon a beauty that has, Ker-

2. Frank Kermode, *Romantic Image* (London: Routledge & Kegan Paul, 1957).

mode says, "the three attributes of integrity, consonance and clarity." Such descriptions, accurate for Yeats, Pater, and other writers associated with them in studies of the symbolist movement, cannot of course be said to apply to all works of art, nor even to some of Yeats's later poems. They suffice to place particular works and to get at conventions that were useful to particular writers. Kermode would never claim he was doing for, say, Auden, what he was doing for Yeats. But he did, by pointing out the operant conventions, identify a sensibility that has influenced all of modern and contemporary art, including Balanchine's work. And since Blackmur was concerned not so consistently with dance but with the poetry of Yeats and Pound and others who worked either in their shadow or against them, that sensibility and those conventions are very much at issue here. Why Blackmur chose largely to ignore them in his study of dance it is hard to say.

Kermode devotes the longest chapter in his book to "The Dancer." But he is concerned less with modernist ballet than with "the freely-moving" figure Heine admired in the street-dancer Mme. Laurence, or with the Jane Avril whose improvisations Toulouse-Lautrec so doted on. These dancers had little in them of the mechanical qualities Blackmur disliked, and it was obviously difficult for their admirers to attribute their successes to technique. They had, in fact, if one is to accept the testimony of infatuated poets and painters, the power to project enigma while seeming utterly detached from the thought of consequence or involvement. Their movement was passionate, not studied, and they seemed in no way to call to mind "the immobility of sculpture." Balanchine may have sought a poise that led even admirers to think in terms of objects in space, but that is not what Yeats and Pater and Arthur Symons had in mind. So the argument goes.

At the same time, much that Kermode says of the image favored by Yeats and others may be observed as well in Balanchine's compositions. We have not the need here to rehearse the refinements of Kermode's argument, but we should at least consider the following points:
1. The Image is "anti-discursive," as may be seen in Symons's evocation of an aesthetic bliss that is as true for the dance as it is for the poem: " 'When the angels talk among themselves,' he wrote, 'their speech is art; for they do not

talk as men do, to discuss matters or to relate facts, but to express either love or wisdom.' ''

2. "Michelangelo proved the intellectual power of mere sinew."

3. Yeats wrote, " 'Did Pater foreshadow a poetry, a philosophy, where the individual is nothing, the flux of the *Cantos* of Ezra Pound, objects without contour . . . , human experience no longer shut into brief lives . . . ?' ''

4. One finds in Pater "the simple form of that cult of the dead face which late, separated from all obvious pathological interest, turns up in Yeats, and in Vorticism."

5. We must think of "Botticelli's concern for rhythm, his indifference to what Yeats, pejoratively, calls 'character.' ''

6. Richard Strauss sought for the lead singer in his *Salome* "some vocal equivalent for that unemotional, disengaged quality—Yeats' word might be 'uncommitted'—which Wilde gave his Salome . . . an innocent, totally destructive malice; beauty inhumanly immature and careless cruelty."

7. Yeats had need of "a poetic image which will resemble the living beauty rather than the marble or bronze. No static image will now serve . . . The Image is to be all movement, yet with a kind of stillness."

To return from this inventory of indifference to Blackmur is to see how close is the Balanchine he describes to providing the image beloved of Yeats. Is not the Balanchine dancer self-contained in the way that Joyce recommended? Is not the beauty of *Concerto Barocco* a function of "integrity, consonance and clarity"? What can these words mean if they do not say what we find in Balanchine? Blackmur insists upon "hysteric exactness," but he speaks also of the work's "expunging the psyche, who is slow, and stubborn. . . ." Though the work may tend toward a perfection, an extraordinary poise that leads one to think of sculptural stasis, its truth remains a truth of movement. If it lacks a "subject," that is only because it cannot be concerned with "matters" or "facts," determined as it is to enact a wisdom that has nothing whatever to do with ordinary sympathies. Blackmur half complains, half wonders over a "proficiency beyond conceivable impulse," but he notes also the way in which the spectator is drawn in, much as Pound's true readers could be moved by representations of an experience "no longer shut into brief lives." Clearly it is not this life or that one hopes to find in Balanchine, not familiarly "conceivable" impulses, but emblems of grace and wholeness. Nor do the circumscriptions seem to come from without in one's experience of the dance performance. The movements of bodies in space compose before the eyes of each spectator a form that seems at once inevitable and unaccountable. The fact that the steps are learned, routines rehearsed, positionings fixed in advance in no way undermines our impression that the various movements find their own form, that the bodies assemble themselves as they are supposed to as much by looking and feeling as by remembering.

More radical, because more sharply at variance with other artistic traditions, is the inventory's almost programmatic emphasis upon the characterless and disengaged. It is easy to see how this focus would create and rationalize the "cult of the dead face" and the tendency to dabble in chic perversions and cruelties. Blackmur doesn't see this sort of chic in Balanchine, but he remarks the absence of sexuality or tenderness. More pointedly, he notes "the scrupulousness of motion so hard it inched on the brittle." He is moved to speak of the impersonal, inhuman aspect of the dancers, all in thrall to the rhythms of the music and the motions they are to go through. Though he misses in them "the living beauty," he does in fact find them beautiful, responding precisely to that quality of hardness that is central to the Image in Yeats's terms. Blackmur resists what seems to him a coldness that is unearned, though it is the nature of the empty "characters" in many modernist works to be "innocent," "careless," "mere sinew." It is not, after all, that Yeats's words seem "careless" but that they express an attraction to something that is cold and austere, something that has no thought of right or wrong but is innocently committed to following out the laws of its nature. Just so do Balanchine's dances—particularly the more formally elegant creations like *Concerto Barocco* and *Jewels*—rigorously pursue their designs without any suggestion of carelessness or improvisation while allowing the dancers to suggest how readily they assume the status of "innocent" vessels, "victims" of a motion to which they submit utterly. Blackmur mistakenly looks for a human habitation in works designed to exorcise human frailty by attaching us to images of speed and adequacy. No wonder he is disappointed. He misses the poignance of the thing because he expects it to feel exactly like the poignance in poets he admires. In Balanchine the poignance is in the recognition that adequacy is a function of enactment. No sooner do the dancers stop enacting what—for the purposes of performance—they are then they are confronted by all that they are not. This confrontation no one of us will avoid as he watches; and as in dance, so in the poem there will be allowance for what cannot be encompassed. "The Image," Kermode reminds us, "is never for long dissociated from the consideration of its cost."

These words open another way into Blackmur's thought and help further to explain what he seeks in the work of art. For if he cannot give himself up to ballet, he does all the same admire Yeats for qualities many of us admire in Balanchine. He has his reservations about Yeats, to be sure, and likes to remind us that the poetry often suffers from an excess of its own characteristic virtues.[3] In all, though, Yeats seems to Blackmur to have counted the costs of his virtues and to have made even the more cumbersome machinery of his imagination work for him. What is the central strength of Yeats's poetry? At its best, it is "a realized, an intensified (not a logical or rhetorical) tautology." Which is to say, it "declares its whatness, its self, with such a concreteness that you can only approach it by bringing abstractions to bear, abstractions from all the concrete or actual experience you can manage to focus." The poem is what it is, and declares its whatness in such a way that the reader will be encouraged to bring to it in his own disciplined way something else. "That is how art attracts richness to itself and reveals its inner inexhaustibleness," Blackmur declares; "that is how art becomes symbolic, . . . how it is autonomous and automotive." The *Concerto Barocco,* in these terms, would be said to have aimed at an autonomy achieved by closing itself off, by enlisting a response that is at most subsequent. In aiming at perfection—something akin to but finally different from tautology—Balanchine alienates the spectator. He invites us to witness, admire, and applaud, but doesn't recommend that we participate in the enactment. Yeats, by con-

3. The major pieces on Yeats are collected in *Language as Gesture* (New York: Harcourt, Brace and Co., 1952).

trast, is said to make a place for us, even as he fashions the unshakably autonomous structure. The poem doesn't need us, but we feel we are given leave to come up to it, provided only that we have some notion of how to behave, of the proper questions we might ask. Yeats reckons the cost of the Image by allowing for the fact that its adequacy will be tried by each reader who approaches it. On the contrary, the *Concerto Barocco* would seem, in Blackmur's sense of it, to repel anything like an intimate approach, to resist the suggestion that it might be more, or other, than it appears to be. Its exactness is tautological, but it refuses to acknowledge cost in the way that Blackmur proposes. In Balanchine ballet, consideration of cost is an afterthought; in Yeats, the consideration is built into the Image. The distinction, for Blackmur, is crucial.

Had Blackmur written more on dance, it might seem plausible to go further with this. But we are interested not so much in his views of Balanchine as in the operations of his mind, his sense of the way art works and impresses itself upon us. More important than his opinion of *Concerto Barocco* are the ways in which he evaluates works of art and teaches us to distinguish one from another. At the heart of his procedures is the concept of tautology, his insistence that the work be everywhere what it is. To be complete, the work need not take it upon itself to strike this pose rather than that. Yeats's austerity, for example, is a necessary condition of autonomy only in his poems. Other kinds of work require other postures. To say that a poem by Yeats manages throughout to be what it is, is to feel that it has concentrated its energies in an entirely concrete way, so that its posture, its expression or containment of affect, seems inevitable. Blackmur asks of the work that it be true to its own project, that it appear to know what it is about. Of course, there is a danger in too much determination; a work that knows all too well what it means to do will unduly limit the effect it can have and the discoveries it can make. These are not matters that will be decided in the same way by all who read poems or study dance. But no one can seriously engage a work of art without considering what it is. This will not often be what it says, or what it means, and anyone who has tried to assign meanings to a Balanchine ballet will know just how remote from meanings certain works can be. Some poets and critics like to say that poems also are remote from the meanings invariably assigned them, that they are what they are and must be known in that way alone. But it is clear that poems made of words will suggest meanings that may more readily be resisted in one's experience of dance or music.

It is also true, of course, that for almost two hundred years poets have wanted to write a poetry so purely expressive that it would achieve the sublime sufficiency of music. Some, in thinking about the poetry of their time, have even gone so far as the music critic who said, in Herbert Read's account, that "he did not mind what language an opera was sung in, so long as he did not understand it." This far Blackmur has never been willing to go. Though he is never hungry for simple meanings, he doesn't pretend to be superior to sense, and he believes that the thing itself is best apprehended by those who know how to pick at it. In poems, the words themselves will be targeted, not because they conceal meanings that beg to be uncovered but because readers will wish to know better what is untranslatable in the poem, what cannot be put in other words. How often does Blackmur, in working with a particular line or image, take satisfaction in being unable to go as far with it as he had hoped: "but I am afraid it will not take analysis," he will tell us. Which is to say that, in moving in on the whatness of the given poem, he will identify that which is irreducible to meaning. His interest is likely to be most exercised at last by "something as primitive as a pulse that the poem dramatizes."

All of this would be arid theorizing if Blackmur did not arrange for us to move with him through various texts. From essay to essay his concerns vary, but he teaches us to be alert always to fundamentals that are as integral to Cummings or Lawrence as to Yeats. In the Yeats essays, there is an emphasis on system, on magic, on the relation between special or occult knowledge and the capacity to read simple words set out simply on the page. But these issues are, in Blackmur's treatment of them, indistinguishable from the others: What is constitutive in a poem by Yeats? What makes it what it is, for example, when it makes no mention of gyres or phases of the moon or other elements of the system elaborated in Yeats's *A Vision*? How does it manage to be true to its own project while implicating all that it is not, bearing witness to what we have called the relevant "cost"? It may be that we are attached to Yeats without considering what that attachment amounts to. Blackmur wants us to be sure of what we are doing when we deliver ourselves into the hands of a real poet. On this score, Allen Tate once accused Blackmur of worrying too much about "the previously established truth of the poet's ideas" in his estimates of Yeats's poetry. But Blackmur treated the ideas as material the poet could or could not use effectively to make the thing that was self-evidently itself. He was attached to Yeats because he found in the poetry a way of accepting Yeats's ideas provisionally, expediently, without feeling called upon to commit himself to them even as he committed himself to the poems. The poems were something else, at their best aloof even from their own ideas. Blackmur doesn't ignore or deny ideas in poetry; he takes them as seriously as the poem asks us to. He assumes there will be more to a good poem than its ideas, but is willing to be persuaded to another view by a poet he respects. By engaging not only the design of the poem—including its statement or appropriation of ideas—but also its project, its implicit thrust, he hopes to identify properly what it is. Yeats may have had a fondness for aristocracy and marching men. He may even have believed that our destiny is controlled by the phases of the moon. His poems, Blackmur would have us agree, do not stand or fall on our willingness to accept these views. We have only to entertain them to give ourselves up to the poems in which they figure, however obscurely or explicitly.

The poetic object, then, is not an idea or a system, any more than a healthy person may be identified wholly by the views he holds. The poem is closer to a process that is everywhere bent upon assuming a finished identity it can never conclusively achieve. Like a thought, it will move from one prospect to another in an effort to resolve its relation to the issue it has felt compelled to address. This issue is not likely to be an issue of grave public moment, or even an issue the poet thought deliberately to address before he set pen to paper. More likely it will be an issue the poem itself discovered as it set out to pursue a vagrant thought or emotion that needed fixing or correcting or fleshing out. Often the thought as elaborated in the poem will be more partial, more narrowly determined than the poet would like it to be, but if the initiating impulse is rich and the poet's responsive apparatus finely tuned, the poem will engage more than the poet knows. Sometimes, in fact, the poem will know more than any reader knows until a Blackmur takes hold of it and puts to it the essential questions. These will have, usually, little to do with ideas if by ideas we mean propositions to which we can assent in the abstract. The essential questions tend instead to consider, as we have said, what the poem is—what it feels like to take possession of it and to be, in turn, possessed; what, also, we can make of it, having arrived at some visceral knowledge of it.

Blackmur proposes, in dealing with Yeats, to consider forms of knowledge that, as he says, "do not fit naturally with the forms of knowledge that ordinarily preoccupy us." But there is more than Yeats's addiction to magic that we must contend with. The magic, systematized as it was by Yeats and "reduced" to a working vocabulary, had its uses, and these other critics had described. Blackmur is determined to take account of the magic without falling prey to the conclusion that in all of the poetry it is constitutive. Essential it might be, as a "mechanics of meaning and value," but not as the central value in itself. For it is Blackmur's contention that a poetic tool, an idea or system or mode of apprehension, may be heuristic, which is to say, "it discovers and performs new feats which could not have been anticipated without it, which it indeed seems to instigate for itself and in the most unlikely quarters." This process of discovery and performance may even go forward best when the mechanics are least visible, when they serve not as an explicit instigation but as a possibility to which only some readers will be alert. Consider, in this regard, "The best lack all conviction, while the worst/Are full of passionate intensity," and determine how essential to the lines is the system that supports them. Yeats invokes the system elsewhere in "The Second Coming," but Blackmur insists we do not need a system "to realize the aptness of the statement to every plane of life in the world about us." We will go on, inevitably, to connect the lines "with the remote body of the poem they illuminate," but the knowledge they make available to us we should be able to grasp more or less at once. If the object of the poem is not magical knowledge but a knowledge of reality—we might do better to call it experience—as Yeats would himself have said, then we must read the quoted lines *as if* they referred to something we can see for ourselves without looking to the prophetic scheme for support.

To see for ourselves the condition described in Yeats's famous lines is, of course, to see through the lenses set in place by the poem. It is to see without yielding entirely to the proposition or to the various poetical conceits that embolden Yeats's assertion. Blackmur speaks of "the aptness of the statement to every plane of life in the world about us," but he does not thereby suggest that all will read the political and cultural conditions of the day in the same way. The aptness has to do with our sense that the central assertions have been plausibly supported, that there is a poetic logic in Yeats's presentation of his vision. The visionary metaphors body forth Yeats's knowledge in a way that makes it available to us. We can say, in thinking of the poem, that we know what it is like to be possessed by the knowledge Yeats wishes us to share. He manages at once to communicate his experience of our collective moment and to represent it with a palpable disinterestedness. The poem's aptness is a function of its capacity to combine passionate utterance—"the best lack all conviction"—with a number of metaphors that seem not to come from Yeats at all. Even the reader who does not thoroughly know the Yeatsian system should feel about the metaphors—the "shape with lion body and the head of a man," the "rocking cradle"—that they have been taken over from some body of knowledge to which all of us have ready access.

The poetic object, here as elsewhere, is not to be identified with the specific prophecy spoken but with the visionary enterprise itself. Blackmur can accept Yeats's ideas because the poet has given them the weight we associate with real things. The ideas are embodied; they are more than the rhetorical assertion that they warrant. The critic knows, quite as the poet knows, that the various figures generated are not real, that they have not the status of objects in the world external to the poem. In fact, theoretical disputes over the reality of words on the page and their reference to an object world never seemed particularly fruitful to Blackmur, who felt he could talk about the experience of a poem without getting involved in arid controversy. In "The Second Coming," the words have the weight of objects *that have been taken for real.* That is the contention. The words summon the authority we identify with a vision that has been honestly tested. The poet has asked himself what would be required by an "uninspired" reader like Blackmur who wished to take seriously a doctrine his intellect found uncongenial. And the question is asked, implicitly, throughout the poem, with an answer that is indistinguishable from the poem itself. For the poem demonstrates that it is possible to think magically, to rely upon a magical knowledge, without submitting to trancelike reverie. It is possible, so Yeats would seem to say, to see the future in the past without abandoning a view of the present moment to which all can attest. And it is possible, finally, to weight the perception of present things by building up a symbolic apparatus that has at once a natural and a "doctrinal reference," quite as Blackmur notes.

Why, then, should Blackmur finally have so much trouble with the poem? For though he tries to defend Yeats, he cannot yield to the poem as he would himself have wished. The trouble extends to other Yeats poems, and though Blackmur thought *Yeats* the greatest English poet in two hundred years, he never learned to feel comfortable about the system, even in poems where it was least apparent. He says, on more than one occasion, that Yeats routinely promises what he cannot deliver. A given poem may dramatize its own failure to come across with the goods, and that is an acceptable though limited thing for a poem to do. Too often, though, dramatization of failure is not the object but the unwitting outcome of a poem that has truly meant to deliver something we can use. In "The Second Coming," Blackmur argues, the magic promises "exact prediction of events in the natural world; and it promises again and again, in different poems, exact revelations of the supernatural." *Promises* is, of course, a peculiar word, and Blackmur recognizes how elusive it can be. To promise is after all not always to foresee how circumstances may alter our chance of doing what we think to accomplish. To promise is to intend or to console in a way for which we cannot always be held strictly accountable. What is the spirit of Yeats's promise in "The Second Coming"? Blackmur notes that in many instances Yeats does no more than confer upon his speculations "the validity of poetic myth." Is the promise of "The Second Coming" such an instance? Blackmur speaks of a "rational defect" and complains that "the thought is not always in the words." This is to say that, because he cannot accomplish as much as he would like with the metaphors that embody and support his prophecy, Yeats is forced to invoke magical knowledge in the form of rhetorical assertion. The assertion may be compelling as rhetoric, but it will be resisted by the reader who needs more than the validity of myth or rhetoric to accept what the poem proposes. If the thought is not in the words that is only because the poet cannot bring himself to impose upon the reader the full certainty of a visionary knowledge the reader will necessarily refuse to take on faith. The rational defect stems from the fact that the thought is not rational and cannot make itself rational by assuming the form of an ordered discourse. Yeats can escape the singular limitations inherent in his procedures only by aiming not at visionary knowledge alone but at something more familiar.

At issue here is the question of authority—not the authority we grant the poet but the authority the poem itself declares. We grant authority to the poet when the poem has legitimately taken hold. This it may accomplish in several different ways, only one or two of which need engage us here in a discussion of the poem's authority. For instance, a poem may be satisfied with a small success, with a modest mastery the reader grants because he has not been confronted with a difficult thought or a painful emotion. Some poems, in fact, aim to do little more than confirm for a particular group or class of readers what they already feel. Blackmur is not ordinarily interested in such poems, though he likes occasionally to show how more ambitious works fall prey to that temptation even while pretending to set down a challenge. The critic takes such works seriously because, in his view, they operate in part as all poems do. "Poetry is so little autonomous from the technical point of view," Blackmur writes, "that the greater part of a given work must be conceived as the manipulation of conventions that the reader will, or will not, take for granted." For example, in a culture for which high literacy is itself but an option among others—even for persons who have been educated—allusion is not likely to have the force it once had. A poet working within an established literary convention may not take for granted the ability even of his educated reader to recognize the operant convention and to grant the authority of its presence.

Nor are literary conventions alone involved. "*Romeo*

and Juliet is less successful today than when produced," Blackmur argues, "because the conventions of honor, family authority, and blood-feud no longer animate and justify the action." This is to say that, where conventions outside the poem—conventions, all the same, on which the poem relies—have no authority in themselves, the language of the poem will be forced to create an authority of its own. If we are resistant on principle to the mastery asserted by mere rhetoric, then we shall be particularly hard to satisfy. Blackmur looks in a Yeats poem for an "edifice of reason" that is "independent of its inspiration" in magic. He understands that Yeats had to create conventions to take the place of all the others that had been eroded and repudiated in his time. But he cannot accept the peculiar Yeatsian conventions simply on the ground that they are ingenious and represent the heroic labors of a great poet. The poems have to establish the conventions without inviting the reader to abandon his own hard-won intelligence. This can be accomplished only when the magic in a given poem ceases to matter as magic. When we look at "The Second Coming" and other such poems, we ask whether "the magical material in these poems is incorporated in them by something like organic reference." No one can answer for certain, but it is possible to learn how to put the question without demanding from the poems what they cannot deliver.

The connection, for Blackmur, between authority and "organic reference" is really at the heart of all his thinking on the status of poetic objects. The magic in Yeats interested the critic so much because we credit Yeats with a major achievement without altogether conceding to him an authority the poems seem eager to claim. Blackmur maintained through all of his career an allegiance to Yeats, but he seems never to have outgrown the resistances elaborated in the early studies. He can give himself over to "Leda and the Swan," after a good deal of misgiving, but he insists that each reader test for himself what is tendentious or mechanical in it. What will the test consider? Primarily, whether material that feels tendentious or mechanical has been kept in to qualify emotion or to take its place. "The poetic approach," Blackmur says, "retains, when it is successful, only what is manifest, the emotion that can be made actual in a form of words that need only to be understood, not argued." One may argue with a conviction that assumes the tone of authority, but the authority laid claim to in a prose "argument" will be different from the poem's authority. The poem's "organic reference" makes possible an authority we grant only to something that is necessary. The poem will be everywhere of a piece, whatever the variety of emotions and ideas it seeks to reconcile. It will be inarguable in the sense that its burden will never be an idea or a point of view but the fact that certain ideas or views or emotions exist and take hold of their possessor in a particular way. The poem's necessary emotion is cluttered—Blackmur's term—, its reality deadened, only when the tendentious or mechanical elements seem their own reason for being, when they demand credence more than provisional acceptance.

Nor is the notion of provisionality at odds with the dimension of necessity we identify in successful poems. This is best demonstrated by Blackmur's approach to Yeats's "The Apparitions." His reading of the poem is intricate and illuminating, as might be expected, but the approach goes well beyond "reading" in the usual sense. He tries to describe the poem and to locate the point at which it brings forward Yeats's vision. He concludes that the vision is effectively communicated because of a "plurisignificance" or "ambiguity" that "is deeper than the particular words of the poem." In fact, Blackmur goes on, "this plurisignificance . . . had as well been secured by other words at the critical places, indeed by the opposite words, so far as superficial, single meanings go." This is an extraordinary observation, so much so that one wonders why it has not been taken up by other critics. What Blackmur contends, in effect, is that necessity in a poem may have more to do with a structure of interaction than with the actual words that do the interacting. One is not therefore encouraged to ignore the actual words or to imagine in every instance that they might just as well be replaced by others. The contention is that the poem describes its own necessity and puts that necessity to the reader in ways that are more or less demanding. The reader who will be equal to it will respond with a re-creative urgency of his own. This urgency may take the form of questions submitted to the poem or of alternative poem- or prose-structures invented to extend, compete with, or take the place of the original without utterly abolishing it. Blackmur was the most fully responsive reader of his time in his willingness to meet the poem fully on its own terms. But he never abandoned his critical sense of how it managed to produce effects that to others seemed perfectly natural, sincere, inevitable. The poem's necessity lay in its capacity to liberate possibility while remaining everywhere of a piece. "The Apparitions" could be said to find its own meanings and to realize itself as a poem by establishing a relation between stanza and refrain. But to leave it at that would have been to impose too heavy an emphasis upon a formal achievement, the matching of one part with another. Blackmur's more radical insight is that the matching is so apt that it tempts a reader to his own "ad libbing around the refrain." The fit must be seen as a provocation and ought to be taken as such in all "poems of this character, which engage possibility as *primum mobile* and last locomotive." How do we know "The Apparitions" is such a poem? By submitting to it and concluding that, for more than half its length, it is a poem in search of an object, a poem that is looking, even as it unfolds, for a way to incarnate its vision. To see the poem in this way is to conclude that the reader, almost as much as the poet, has a work to do if the poem is to be granted its own necessary thrust. "One tends to let poems stay too much as they are," Blackmur says. "Do they not actually change as they are read? Do they not, as we feel them intensely, fairly press for change on their own account?"

We are quite ready to agree, no doubt, that poems seem to change as they are read. But do they "actually change"? What does it mean to say that they "fairly press for change on their own account"? Blackmur can mean only that they invite us to imagine them as other than they are in order to apprehend them more securely as what they are. The poetic object is not a thing but a process that can be experienced only if one is alert to its potential modalities. In "The Apparitions" the words would seem to do whatever they are supposed to do. But as soon as we determine to *say* what the poems do, we see that they are but a "notation," that we care about a "gesture" of connection more than the words that compose the gesture. We can believe that Yeats has found the best words possible for the particular occasion without agreeing to content ourselves with them as they appear on the page. In the third stanza of "The Apparitions," Blackmur says, the words "drag after them into being their own opposites, not for contradiction but for development."

> When a man grows old his joy
> Grows more deep day after day,
> His empty heart is full at length,
> But he has need of all that strength
> Because of the increasing Night
> That opens her mystery and fright.
> *Fifteen apparitions have I seen;*
> *The worst a coat upon a coat-hanger.*

I confess to having read this poem on a number of occasions without feeling Blackmur's "opposites" dragged into being. Perhaps that is why the poem never seemed to me as rich as it has since I allowed Blackmur to open it up for me. What the critic advises here, in a modest way, can only be called poetical thinking. A poet knows that in a poem like "The Apparitions" what counts is the retrospective force the refrain lines will cast back upon the stanzas that precede them. The reader will be moved not by the particular proposition but by the way in which the speaker is gripped and drawn to summarize the experience of old age. We don't have to know, Blackmur says, which came first, the stanzas or the refrain. We know that in their interaction is "the cry, the gesture, the metaphor of identity, which as it invades the words, and whichever words, is the poem we want." According to this logic, we are within our rights to follow out the several opposites poised to invade the poem: "let us ad lib the stanza quoted above," Blackmur encourages, "so that instead of joy growing more deep it grows less, so that the full heart grows empty, and remark that he has need of all that room—the room of emptiness, it will be—precisely

> Because of the increasing Night
> That opens her mystery and fright.

But let us not stop there. Could not the night diminish as well as increase; could it not, for the purposes of the achieved poem, close as well as open?"

To ad lib in this way, of course, is to see ever more surely that the poem is not about the joy that old men feel as they approach their end. In fact, any reader might well disagree with the proposition, without feeling called upon to resist the poem. The truth of the poem is in its particular adequacy, which is an adequacy of metaphor to portrait. Thus we say that, having been forced three times to confront "a coat upon a coat-hanger," we come to accept it as a final apparition of a man grown old. The poem claims an identity, and its truth is the way in which it is made to seem irresistible to the speaker. To try the poem by changing key words, as Blackmur does, is to discover that the identity remains. Whether the heart grows empty or full, it is a heart that will be responsive to the approach of night. And that night, whether it is said to diminish or increase, will be enough to sustain the projection of the self as apparition. Blackmur entertains "opposites" because he wishes to be driven toward what is essential in Yeats's vision. His reading avoids any suggestion of easy contradiction because he works with a poem that so obviously searches out its truth. He doesn't, in his essay, quote the first two stanzas of "The Apparitions," but the reader of the poem will agree at once that the poem opens and seems at first to move on without knowing quite what it wishes to discover. Only the refrain at the end of the stanzas indicates that the speaker is possessed by something he will have to find a way to communicate. With sheer possibility so evidently underwriting the poem, the critic is free to work with it as he will.

This is not always a proper approach. In fact, Blackmur would often say that the best poems are so self-evidently what they are that they leave us with nothing to say about them. He did not insist upon this as an irrefutable criterion of poetic success, but he did come back to the point again and again in his many essays. Organic reference, he would contend, can be so thoroughly managed that one cannot for a moment doubt the authority that rings in an utterance. Conceptually, as also in terms of execution, *Madame Bovary* is so much a unity that even the most disparate particulars "must be felt together to be felt justly." To acknowledge that perfect unity is not to refrain from devoting an essay to the novel, but one knows that the criticism is necessary largely because of unfortunate developments in our habits of reading and thinking. If we cannot readily perceive unities for ourselves, if we are inclined to resist them where they are apparent, we must be instructed in new habits of thinking. Blackmur's late essays on Flaubert and Joyce, among others,[4] mean to be instructional in this sense but take up too many other issues to be as useful as the earlier essays on the poets. Whatever our feeling about this, we cannot ignore the continuity of critical attention. And so it is well to consider the kind of poem Blackmur thought authoritative in the light of observations he made not only about other kinds of successful poems—like "The Apparitions"—but about works of fiction.

The essay on *Ulysses* is particularly instructive. There the critic argues that at least one great work of literature may more properly be addressed by a scholar than by a reader or critic. For "the élan of reading" we substitute—in the form of various guidebooks—"the vice of scholarship." Why? Because most of us have, as readers, no ready means of access to *Ulysses*. This comes as no surprise to literary people, but even the Joyce experts may need to take notice of Blackmur's larger point: that the book itself is "a series of arbitrary aesthetic, technical, and intellectual measures" undertaken by a writer who knew exactly what was required. Joyce, in Blackmur's account of him, constructed his novel in response to what he saw as a colossal breakdown in the relation between the ideal and the actual in modern life. Bereft of institutional, aesthetic or spiritual supports for the work he wished to do, Joyce built into the very texture of his novel his sense of bereavement. By creating an obsessively orderly work, Joyce called constant attention to his arbitrary imposition of that order. All of the many orders summoned—with varying degrees of explicitness—in the novel, he summons "as if they were aesthetic, images or stresses rather than summaries or concepts of the actual." Since we have no sense of the actual as reliant upon ulterior supports of any kind, since we have lost contact with the various orders that propose an ideal foundation for the projects we assume, we have no way of dealing with a compulsive impulse to order. Without the assistance of scholars and guidebooks, a work like *Ulysses* must seem to us impenetrable or "frivolous," a declaration of "impotent" longing. "Joyce had none of that conviction which is the inward sense of outward mastery." So Blackmur concludes.

4. Included in his volume *Eleven Essays in the European Novel* (New York: Harcourt, Brace and World, 1964).

Joyce wrote one of the world's great books because he was equal to his own sense of loss and knew how to dramatize his combat against the specter of his own impotence.

Joyce's combat had everything to do with the images of authority he sought and failed to find in modern life. Lacking those necessary images, he constructed an aesthetic substitute that might be taken for the sign of mastery others like him missed in the crumbling belief-systems around them. But Joyce's ordered aesthetic substitutes could not, in Blackmur's estimation, succeed in creating the necessary response. "Perhaps all art is imposed order," he wrote, "but it ought to be the order called for by the substance in terms of the governing concepts of those imaginations which are not aesthetic." Had Joyce been able to find in his society some semblance of the authority images and spiritual forms he sought, he might have been able to invest in his characters an actuality we should be able to acknowledge as our own. Instead, he gave us figures who move well beyond our grasp of them, figures to be interpreted and made use of. Joyce's Bloom may be, as Blackmur says, "a way of expressing what the conditions of life are," but the expression of those conditions in the novel as a whole suffers from the problem that so afflicts the other main character, Stephen Dedalus. Stephen, Blackmur argues, has a hard time making contact with the actual conditions of life because he "can only undertake it independently and intellectually." Joyce has only the force of his own brilliance and ingenuity and desire to sustain him in a project that should have meant more to us had it been underwritten by another kind of authority.

There is no need to argue with Blackmur about *Ulysses*. Much that he says about the novel is worth considering at least, and the rest of his essay is so much in the nature of an ecstatic gloss that it repels close analysis. What is most important for our purposes is Blackmur's notion of a text whose authority is nowhere to be taken for granted, an author who is "omnivorous of detail because without his authorities he has no principles of economy." The critique of Joyce elaborates in this way, implicitly, a standard of adequacy that can best be realized in a certain kind of lyric poem. Yeats wrote that sort of poem, though more often he was tempted to do things like "The Apparitions" or more ambitious works requiring an interpretative apparatus like the Joyce guidebooks. Blackmur does not feel called upon to rank the kinds of poems as greater or lesser achievements. He is committed to distinguishing one kind from another and to indicating the different reader responses invited by them. "The Apparitions" invited a particular kind of response associated with the nimble following out of possibility. Another poem by Yeats, "A Deep-Sworn Vow," requires something else. It is, in Blackmur's terms, a poem in which the words are "in an ultimate sense their own meaning." To read it is to be tempted to the view that "possibly all poetry should be read as this poem is read, and no poetry greatly valued that cannot be so read." It is a simple poem, and the more tempting for that fact as well.

> Others because you did not keep
> That deep-sworn vow have been friends of mine;
> Yet always when I look death in the face,
> When I clamber to the heights of sleep,
> Or when I grow excited with wine,
> Suddenly I meet your face.

Blackmur refuses to make much of the poem. It seems to him to go about as far as a poem can go in the direction of "absolute autonomy and self-perfection." He remembers, though, that not all poems can so readily depend upon a sharing of operant conventions by poet and readers. Where the sharing is incomplete, where the conventions are not clearly accepted by all parties, the poem is likely to show more strain, to seem less self-sufficient or complete. Effects will appear to be won more by manipulation than by a simple statement of emotion. The dimension of metaphor may not be any more deliberately inscribed than it appears to be in "A Deep-Sworn Vow," but it will invite the kind of analysis that poem resists. In his fine book on *W. B. Yeats: Self-Critic*,[5] Thomas Parkinson tries to perform a modest analysis of "A Deep-Sworn Vow" only to demonstrate that there isn't much of consequence to say. The attempt to say more than is required, in fact, is likely to tempt the reader to go against the grain of a plausible response in which all attentive readers may share. The Blackmur who believes that Yeats's poem says very satisfactorily exactly what it

5. Thomas Parkinson, *W. B. Yeats: Self-Critic* (Berkeley: University of California Press, 1971).

means to say would have to repudiate Parkinson's observation that, if "the first two lines present the behaviour of the speaker in the world of time," then "the last four present his vision of eternal, or at least recurrent, value." To speak of "eternal" or even of "recurrent" value in such a poem is to assimilate it all too easily to the perspective of Yeats's other poems. It is to say that, because Yeats had much to do with questions of value, he was positively bound to be addressing them in everything he wrote. Similarly, the reader who knows Yeats, who has struggled with the Byzantium poems and the other anthology pieces, will simply have to read "A Deep-Sworn Vow" as a minor variation generated from the poet's larger concerns. The fact that no ordinary reader will wish to read the poem in that way, and that it is the ordinary reader precisely whom Yeats wished to touch, will count for nothing in the analysis of so determined a critic as Parkinson.

Nor is that all he shows us in his determination to analyze Yeats's poem. He shows also that the attempt to account for the poem's success in critical terms is likely to produce more questions than it can answer. "The factual offhand character of 'have been friends of mine,' " Parkinson writes, "is matched by the kinetic suggestiveness of 'clambered' and 'grow excited.' " An interesting observation, but doubtful. The words "have been friends of mine" may hardly be said to constitute a "factual offhand" statement. On the contrary, the words seem calculated to acknowledge something without having to say it in so many words. Yeats is not, after all, speaking of friendship in this poem but of the betrayal of vows that are taken by lovers. The words "have been friends of mine" describe the speaker's own falling away from the perfect constancy he'd earlier conceived. They resonate with the full weight of all that he will not say. To speak of them as "factual" or "offhand" is to miss the qualities of obliqueness and tense restraint built into them. Looking at the words as I have suggested, one sees that they are not perhaps "matched" by "the kinetic suggestiveness" of the following terms, but clarified. Parkinson wishes to address the fact that "the two sections of the poem are held together," and to this end he has to speak of unity of tone and to claim that "if the poem were changed at any point—radically changed—the rest of the poem would also require radical change." Blackmur clearly agrees, but doesn't see that it is necessary for the critic to characterize what should be self-evident features of a poem that is likely to be violated in being translated into another mode of discourse. This may seem peculiar, coming from a critic who was so often accused of splitting hairs and murdering to dissect. But Blackmur thought he knew what criticism was, and was not, good for, and he never intended to allow the critical commentary to compete with the spirit of the original text. If that text clearly did not need to be illuminated by commentary, if it was its own more than adequate illumination, criticism might well constitute a violation.

An "outside" observer would be well within his rights to ask, at this point, what made Blackmur so sure that Yeats's poem provided its own adequate illumination. If so experienced a reader as Parkinson found himself in difficulty, why would not this be the case with most other readers? Blackmur was no theorist, and so it is fair to say that, depending on when and in what circumstance the question was put to him, he might have answered in several different ways. The critic Richard Foster showed, in his study of Blackmur's progress "From Criticism to Mysticism," that Blackmur had a hard time with concepts like *reason* and *judgment,* and used them variously to help him into and out of various literary puzzles. Challenged about the self-evident nature of "A Deep-Sworn Vow," Blackmur would have had to invoke a special conception of reason to explain his certainty. Foster quotes a sentence from the 1954 essay "Between the Numen and the Moha" that reads: "It is art, by ravishing reason's judgment, that reminds reason of its role." In this sense, a reading like Parkinson's may be said to rely too explicitly on judgment when the poem at issue ought to have been permitted to work its magic. Even to speak of the poem's unity of tone—to adopt, in other words, what are clearly judgment-terms—is in this view to represent misleadingly the experience the poem enables. Does the experience of the poem include a recognition of the tonal unity achieved in the integration between parts one and two? Blackmur would say that the thought of unity does not figure in at all, that if we are pressed we shall have instead to note in the poem a shift of tone that is so perfectly managed that it never presents itself to us as an issue at all. For is there not, in the first two lines of Yeats's poem, a note of hurt and accusation mingled with the more obvious element of restraint? And are not the succeeding lines very different in the tone of forgiveness and reconciliation they seek to establish? Blackmur is right. Judgment-terms ought not to color one's account of the experience of this poem. Judgment plays a role in one's response, no doubt, but the proper response will remind reason, quite as Blackmur says, of its subordinate role.

To think poetically, then, for Blackmur, is to be tactful, to be able to restrain one's own various faculties as they are asked to respond to objects in the world. Poetic objects especially exercise those capacities of tact and restraint by addressing us provisionally, by inviting us to think not of whole classes of things but of specific objects that discover their own laws as they unfold. The business of the poet, in this sense, is to think poetically so as to allow objects to emerge that do truly generate their own necessities. Failed poets are less tactful than they ought to be and so impose upon their poems laws of their own ulterior devising or laws taken over from the tradition in which they have chosen to work. Such poems seem not to be self-generating; always they refer not alone to something outside themselves—that may be all to the good—but to designs and principles to which they are subordinate. Blackmur's critique of Balanchine, with which we began this chapter, accused the artist of imposing upon his own "poetic" objects the heavy hand of his own technical devices and certainties. Yeats, by contrast, may be said to have created a perfectly autonomous work that yet makes room for "chaos," for that sense of indeterminacy or ambivalence that constitutes the presence of a human motive. The authority of Yeats's better poems is the authority we cannot but acknowledge in works that know what they are about and, at the same time, what they cannot explain or answer for. It is an authority we find as well in Blackmur's best essays, if not in his poems. For he wrote, as Denis Donoghue rightly says, "not to enlarge the scope of his knowledge but to practice different ways of knowing things." And fully to accept these "different ways of knowing things" is to accept that we had best grant to deserving objects a wholeness, an otherness that can belong only to things we honor as continuously enacting a reality of their own. Blackmur honors, it is clear, only those objects that refuse to stop enacting their own sufficient reason for being. What seemed to his intellectual opponents an inability to stick to the point of his discourse was a function of his insistence that the point was always a moving target.

III. CONTENT IN POETRY

"All that can ever actually be brought into the discussion of a poem is its technical aspects. Which happens in all but the best poetry to be very near the whole of it."—R.P. Blackmur, "The Method of Marianne Moore," in *Language as Gesture*, p. 265.

W hen Delmore Schwartz in 1938 accused Blackmur of "abstraction, incompleteness, and omission," he was calling into question those aspects of Blackmur's procedure that had seemed least susceptible to challenge. Blackmur had never pretended to do the things earlier critics thought important, and he was careful to indicate how partial and provisional his approaches were. But within the limits he'd assigned, he meant to create the impression that he had considered all that was needed to give a fair account of the works at hand. It was clear that a more detailed account of Eliot's Christianity might be provided, or that Yeats's politics might be examined more scrupulously. Someone would want, no doubt, to discuss Stevens's ideas and to track them to their sources. But Blackmur, as poet-critic, had other things to do. He was as interested as anyone else in ideas and was never inclined to ignore the substance of the poem. But his critical function was to enact the experience of reading, to respond to the poetic object in the way the object invited him to do. The concern with Eliot's Christianity or Yeats's politics would have to be invoked at a much later stage, after the poem had been appropriated. One could not avoid the thought of Christianity in first reading "Ash Wednesday," but engagement of doctrinal issues could be deferred even as one registered the prospect of taking them on. A poem that demanded at once to be read as idea, to be taken as the statement of a content, was by that measure alone to be discounted and put aside. Schwartz's criticism of Blackmur—he is "most often training his gaze on the form and quickly summarizing the substance in a general statement," as if the substance were of little consequence—superficially describes the practice without getting at the heart of Blackmur's enterprise. He trained his gaze not on the form but on the poem. And what was the poem if not "the discrete parts—sentences, phrases, single words" that Schwartz accuses Blackmur of stressing too insistently? Those sentences and words had something to say, no doubt, but more important was the gesture they were designed to enact. This it was the business of the critic to apprehend and to evaluate. Was it a gesture worth enacting? What burden of meaning could be embodied in that gesture, which was more than the statement of an idea? Presuming at one point to speak for Blackmur as for himself, Schwartz writes that "a poem is successful when its words represent its substance." Exactly. And for Blackmur it was evident that, while many others were capable of addressing substance, few knew how to deal with the representation of substance when that representation was something more than simple statement. He would get at the substance of the thought of his time by examining poems with the eyes of a poet and the disciplines of a rational skeptic.

The most dangerous thing a poet could do, in Blackmur's view, was to rely upon ideas to do his thinking for him. Though he did not petition to have the words "no ideas but in things" inscribed in every English department textbook, he did believe—with James and Eliot—that educated people were as likely as anyone else to be "violated" by ideas. Even great poets were susceptible, and readers who identified the success of their work with the ideas they seemed to promote would only fail to read the poems properly. They might even encourage the poets to think of themselves as responsible primarily to those arresting ideas. Many readers in the 1930s and 1940s, encouraged by Eliot's essays, discussed his poems as statements of Christian ideas. Insofar as his ideas had hardened into fully formed beliefs, it seemed plausible to think of the poems as vehicles deliberately constructed for the dissemination of the true faith. Schwartz knew as well as Blackmur that good poems didn't work that way and gave as evidence the fact that "we do not reject a poet because of his beliefs (*qua* beliefs), although we can condemn the *effect* of his beliefs on his knowledge of facts and his representation of them." Though he worried over Blackmur's excessive reliance on form, Schwartz knew that Blackmur's "method" was proof against the seduction of ideas, and he allowed himself to hope that the method would continue to spread. If it did, Blackmur's notion of the poetic mind as "the whole mind" would subvert the view of poems laboring in the service of particular ideas to which they were inflexibly bound.

The representation of substance did not seem to Blackmur an esoteric preoccupation. It might enable the examination and celebration of mysteries, but it would all the same provide a model of the mind at work that would be more or less familiar to all of us. In fact, even when the substance seemed resolutely unfamiliar, it might be recommended to our interest by the way in which it was handled in a poem. Because Eliot's Christianity was not an expression of a world view most of his readers could share, the poet was required to work through it dramatically in order to make it seem interesting. This he could not have done successfully if he did not have a dramatic relation to the material. Technique was one thing, conviction another. Blackmur's concentration upon the elements of technical mastery did not prevent him from attending as well to the question of conviction and the substance of the ideas at issue.[1] Eliot seemed to him a great poet because he never permitted his ideas or beliefs to get in the way of his desire to see and to reflect. Reflection was given a certain shape and direction by belief, but the rhythms of reflection were finally responsible more to Eliot's character and temperament than to any particular idea. This Blackmur attempted to show by constructing a portrait of Eliot's mind and relating that portrait to the catholic mind in general. The procedure risked abstraction and could be saved only by being forced finally to confront not the catholic mind in general, but Dante. The critic, like Schwartz, who doubted that Blackmur's method could bear to dwell upon substance as it handled form, had only to examine the operation of the method in the essay "Unappeasable and Peregrine" to put his doubts to rest. Here are two passages, the first fully illuminating and substantive but tending toward abstraction, the second a more concrete working through of the dominant insight. At issue is the quality of conviction in Eliot's *Four Quartets:*[2]

It is because Eliot's mind is both circular and dramatic that it

1. The two major essays on Eliot appear in *Language as Gesture* (New York: Harcourt, Brace and Co., 1952).
2. The excerpts are taken from "Unappeasable and Peregrine," *Language as Gesture.*

has had to resort so much to analogy; and it is because his mind, as sensibility, is a great onion of analogy that he has had to resort to so many patterns and frames of experience. If you think of the Mediterranean mind, it is one thing, which is not the same as the northern mind, catholic or not. The northern catholic mind would seem to require (since it contains so much more material which has not been incorporated into the Graeco-Christian rationale) a greater recourse to analogy to explain, or express, its own content to itself. This is only a suspicion, and only thrown out. But in any case, the Christian mind is never the whole mind, though the whole mind may aspire to be Christian, and it is one way of construing the Christian poet's task to make something—to make as much as he can—of the struggle of the whole mind to enact that aspiration. That is one way of accounting for what Eliot is up to in these poems. He has to discover what it is in that mind which struggles, and he has to find ways—analogies—by which he can keep his discoveries present. He has to keep present all those creations other than Christian, all those conditions of life other than human, which affect his sensibility and press into his behavior.

In Dante there are many languages of the mind conspicuously and consciously at work. In Eliot, though there are other modes working, a predominance of the work is done in the language of the words themselves. We deal largely with what has got into the language *as* words, relatively little with what the words call on . . . We are left with what the words will bear and with reminders of what the language will not bear . . . It seems, looking back, that with Dante the great rebellious troubles of unbelief fed and strengthened his belief, but that with Eliot there is a struggle between belief and unbelief in which each devours the other, except at the moment of desperation . . . In Dante the Love still moved the sun and the other stars; and there is everywhere the continuous declaration of indestructible human identity. In Eliot there is the choice of pyre or pyre, of consumption or consummation, in either case a destruction. It would seem that the purgation destroys that which was to have been purged, and that refinement is into nothingness.

At least this isthe sort of judgment into which we should be pushed by the ''doctrine'' of the poem, if we had to accept the doctrine by itself and without benefit of the images of permanent analogy to which it clings and with which it corrects itself.

Were this a study of Eliot we should need to test more thoroughly what Blackmur says against the passages he cites as support. In fact, though, not much of the argument about Eliot's Christianity can be properly tested in this way. The reader who expects New Critics to rely everywhere on quotation will be surprised to find very little specific support for the reading of Eliot's Christianity. Why? Because Blackmur expects the reader to be so familiar with the general thrust of the *Four Quartets* that he will not need to be reminded by quotation of the kind of poem it is. Also because, in speaking of Eliot, the critic must feel he is dealing with a poet who knew what he was doing and could not usually be "caught" pretending to do something that was contradicted by the action of words in his own poem. Blackmur wished to place and to evaluate Eliot in a way the poet could not do for himself, but he never felt he could do this by searching through the *Four Quartets* to set Eliot against himself. Quotation might serve to focus an aspect of Eliot's tone or his resort to a particular locution. It might even show what Blackmur saw in a passage of "Burnt Norton": the "effect of behavior rising into belief, as it were altering the experience of belief if not the belief itself." But it had to be difficult to isolate in a passage or two the full nature of Eliot's Christian mind. Blackmur attempted to show by analysis and argument what in any case no one would accept with perfect ease: that Eliot's Christianity was very much a reflection both of his time and of his own temper.

Does this pass for substance? Is Blackmur interested in Eliot's Christianity for itself or simply as an item to be gotten through on the way to a critical estimation of the verse? Schwartz had asked whether, in taking hold of the words of a poem, Blackmur had ever been sufficiently interested in the "access of knowledge" the poem enabled. *Four Quartets* would have been said, in this sense, to make available a knowledge of Christianity that was at most incidental to Blackmur's critical concerns. So far as we can tell, Eliot's Christianity is not of primary interest to the critic. He is not, it seems, considering the Christian option for himself. Neither does he have the disinterested or objective passion of the cultural historian who wants to see what truth can possibly inhere in the Christian doctrine now that its cultural supports have mostly been taken away. He feels that he is working toward an understanding of Eliot's Christianity, but he doesn't think of Christianity as the myth of Christ or as the incarnation of myth in ritual. He knows, of course, that Christianity is myth, and ritual, and an entire body of doctrine and tradition, but to him it is more importantly an intellectual discipline and a mode of being. He cares about it less as a system of belief than as a process of thought. Does this mean he has no patience with doctrine or system? It means only that, for Blackmur, good poems are not about doctrine or system. The poet may intend to celebrate or to rationalize his relation to a doctrine, but that is to do more than furnish an account of the doctrine itself. No doubt, the critic may find it necessary to speak about the doctrine in a more extended way than Blackmur chooses to. There is a good deal to be said for the approach of George Santayana in his famous essays on "The Poetry of Christian Dogma" and "The Homeric Hymns."[3] Blackmur's practice does not amount to a repudiation of philosophic or historical criticism. It is an assertion of a certain kind of primacy and is in that sense ideally suited to the treatment of work by the critic's contemporaries. For Blackmur, the reader's primary relation must be to a text. If the text relies upon, or wishes to rationalize, a doctrine, the reader will have to find a way of coming into relation with that doctrine. He will bear in mind, however, that the doctrine cannot be the sufficient reason for being of the text if that text happens to be a poem. Blackmur's criticism is designed to ensure that readers will learn how to keep a proper distance from the doctrine without refusing to look at it. A Santayana will be less interested in the experience of the poem—though on occasion he can do well with that too—and more involved in issues of religious mystery and sanction. For Santayana, the poem is interesting or not depending upon the degree in which it bears witness to a doctrinal possibility the philosopher takes to be crucially important.

A number of literary theorists in our time have attempted to distinguish between the one approach and the other by giving them different names. The best of these theorists, E. D. Hirsch, goes back to the origins of the

3. Both in Santayana's *Interpretations of Poetry and Religion* (New York: Charles Scribner's Sons, 1900; reprint ed., New York: Harper & Brothers, 1957).

science of hermeneutics to locate the distinction between what he calls *interpretation* and *criticism*.[4] Following the example of August Boeckh, he identifies in interpretation "the construction of textual meaning as such; it explicates (*legt aus*) those meanings, and only those meanings, which the text explicitly or implicitly represents. Criticism, on the other hand, builds on the results of interpretation." As the two activities are different, he goes on, so will their objects differ: "The object of interpretation is textual meaning in and for itself and may be called the *meaning* of the text. The object of criticism, on the other hand, is that meaning in its bearing on something else (standards of value, present concerns, etc.), and this object may therefore be called the *significance* of the text." By this distinction, we see, Blackmur would be concerned with meaning, Santayana with significance. The one would be content to root out local meanings or intentions and to assign a value to the text that would measure only how well it had achieved the goals it set itself. The other would take for granted the local meanings or, after working at them more or less dutifully, would gratefully pass on to the big questions, assigning significance as a measure of the poem's ability to illuminate our lives.

The problem with all of this is that a good critic is likely to be skilled in both activities, and that interpretation rarely proceeds—outside the undergraduate classroom—without thought of significance. Why would the interpreter go on with his work if he did not feel that meaning had ultimately a "bearing on something else"? It is legitimate to think of stages in the appropriation of a text, not of fully separate or exclusive procedures. There are practitioners, no doubt, who carry over into their articles and academic books the altogether elementary and self-limiting interpretative procedures of the classroom. But it is not with such interpreters that Hirsch is really concerned, and none of the New Critics who came to prominence in the 1930s operated in that way. Blackmur's small interest in the "knowledge" that might be taken from a poem and isolated in a critical commentary was not a function of a decision to leave questions of significance

4. See E. D. Hirsch's "Objective Interpretations," in *On Literary Intention*, ed. David Newton-De Molina (Scotland: Edinburgh University Press, 1976).

to others. He believed he was as interested in significance as anyone could be, and his consideration of Eliot's Christianity, for example, was part of an attempt to see what a Christian mind could be and mean in a time like ours. A Santayana could quite properly address the significance of an avowedly Christian poetry by arguing for a conception of religion as a great imaginative, even a poetic, discipline. Blackmur might have done the same had he been inclined to associate the good of man and the health of civilization with religious conviction. He tended, instead, to value certain qualities of thought that might belong equally to Christians and to nonbelievers. He knew that the content of a thought mattered, that the content could even determine how nimble or mature the thought might be. But he could not feel that the content of a thought was sufficient by itself to give the thought validity. Validity was the primary measure of significance, and it depended upon the responsiveness of the thought to all that it could not immediately avow or take in. The content of a thought, a belief, or a doctrine was valid not because it could claim adherents or because the critic himself found in it a profound consolation. Validity could be assigned only if the particular content had been appropriated by a whole mind that knew how to register, along with its conviction, that which it could not hold or use. Blackmur's interpretation of a text was a way of discovering what the mind responsible for that text was good for. He was serious about the texts he treated because they were the incarnations of mind, the best way Blackmur knew of penetrating the mind of another. The only way he could make contact with that mind was by making himself a responsive interlocutor, a reader who could come at the text with the requisite tact and, where appropriate, forebearance. To seek to summarize the meanings of the text, to treat its content as so many ideas or beliefs that might be selfishly possessed or carried off, was to violate a mind by supposing it was but a single concern or obsession.

There were, to be sure, writers who were themselves avid to be violated by a simple idea. This we have already indicated. And it was the work of such writers Blackmur most thoroughly repudiated and exposed. But before considering what it took to "expose" such writers, it may be useful to go on a little further with the question of content and the proper critical relation to it. It is easy, of course, to find examples of writers who, having no respect for the thought embodied in a text, also have no respect for their own thought and the finer discriminations it may be trained to make. But we can also find gifted critics who exemplify a relation to content so different from Blackmur's that it may be instructive to compare them. The English writer George Orwell was a first-rate political and cultural critic who, in addition, wrote a number of extraordinary literary essays. One of these, surprisingly, he devoted to Eliot's quartets, or to the first three, at any rate. It is an instructive performance.[5] Orwell concludes, in trying to explain why he is so little taken with Eliot's later work, that there must be "a deterioration in Mr. Eliot's subject matter." One cannot for a moment imagine Blackmur saying such a thing, but he would surely have been curious to see how Orwell arrives at his judgment. What Orwell does, in brief, is to quote two passages, one from "The Dry Salvages," another from an earlier poem. He then summarizes what he takes to be the dominant attitude or view of things expressed in each fragment. He prefers the earlier poem because its view of death is what a sensible man should call a sensible view. Orwell finds resentment of death and a sense that, however bad things may be in the world, life is surely to be preferred over death. The later poem, on the contrary, is said to resign itself too readily to everlasting uncertainty, to a view of life and death as somehow equally shadowy and equivocal experiences. The assumption underlying these observations is that the better poem will unquestionably express a more acceptable view of its subject, which is death.

More instructive still, by way of contrasting Blackmur's usual practice, is Orwell's summary statement of his position on *Four Quartets*. In fact, his essay is all what we should call summary statement, and the fact that we can speak of it as elaborating a position says a good deal about the gap that separates this sort of thing from Blackmur. What are the *Quartets* "about," Orwell asks, and goes on to speculate about the meaning of life in Eliot: "It is not a meaning one feels inclined to grow lyrical about," he says. "If one wants to deal in antitheses, one might say that the later poems

5. Included in *The Collected Essays, Journalism, and Letters of George Orwell,* ed. Sonia Orwell and Ian Angus, vol. 2 (New York: Harcourt, Brace and World, 1968). The essay was written in 1942.

express a melancholy faith and the earlier ones a glowing despair. They were based on the dilemma of modern man, who despairs of life and does not want to be dead, and on top of this they expressed the horror of an over-civilized intellectual confronted with the ugliness and spiritual emptiness of the machine age." In these observations, Orwell goes about as far as Blackmur would permit him to go in describing Eliot's vision from without. The critic stands aside and delivers a version of Eliot that makes little or no reference to the poetic circumstance in which the vision takes shape. Nor are references to early poems and late poems sufficient to designate the poetic circumstance, which Blackmur would try in his own criticism to appropriate and enter into even as he discussed the content of the vision. What Orwell describes is Eliot's position, such as he takes it to be, and that position he cannot refrain from responding to with a position of his own. If Blackmur refused, as a critic of poetry, to identify content with positions, with a vision held and formulated in isolation from the dynamics of the poem, that was because he could not wish to respond to poems with positions of his own. To do so would have been to read Eliot's *Quartets* with the common-sense rationalism of Orwell. That insistence upon plain common sense and downrightness had its uses, to be sure, but one had only to see it applied to Eliot to know that there are some things it cannot do. Consider:

> The trouble is that conscious futility is something only for the young. One cannot go on "despairing of life" into a ripe old age. One cannot go on and on being "decadent," since decadence means falling and one can only be said to be falling if one is going to reach the bottom reasonably soon. Sooner or later one is obliged to adopt a positive attitude towards life and society.

Or the following:

> You have a man who does not really *feel* his faith, but merely assents to it for complex reasons. It does not in itself give him any fresh literary impulse. At a certain stage he feels the need for a "purpose," and he wants a "purpose" which is reactionary and not progressive; the immediately available refuge is the Church, which demands intellectual absurdities of its members; so his work becomes a

continuous nibbling round those absurdities, an attempt to make them acceptable to himself . . . Mr. Eliot speaks also of the intolerable wrestle with words and meanings. The poetry does not matter. I do not know, but I should imagine that the struggle with meanings would have loomed smaller, and the poetry would have seemed to matter more, if he could have found his way to some creed which did not start off by forcing one to believe the incredible.

Orwell wants to give the poet his due. He even concedes that poets may make good use of ideologies that are, in themselves, abhorrent. "Neither feudalism nor indeed Fascism is necessarily deadly to poets," he writes, "though both are to prose-writers." In responding as he does to Eliot, he wants to believe that he objects not to Eliot's views but to the absence of "any fresh literary impulse." But why, then, the emphasis upon Eliot's attitudes and convictions? Why the attempt to write off Eliot's belief as so much dabbling in nonsense? Is it true that the *Quartets* represent the Church in a way no sensible person can take seriously?

By responding to the content of the *Quartets* as if Eliot had been trying to make the rest of us "believe the incredible," Orwell misstates the central problem of the poem. That problem Blackmur describes as the representation of a doctrine that can only be redeemed by "images of permanent analogy to which it clings and with which it corrects itself." The poet's business, in this sense, is to permit the mind to enact its relation to a doctrine to which it submits even as it generates new possibilities of relation that must also be addressed. The reader is not asked to yield or submit as the poet wishes to submit. If he were, Orwell would be correct to complain of a "deterioration in Mr. Eliot's subject matter." For submission to doctrine is not a sufficiently active prospect to serve as the object of a living poem. Blackmur would surely have agreed that good poems bear the marks of a "fresh literary impulse," but he would also have wondered why Orwell thought to get at such things by worrying over the "intellectual absurdities" demanded by the Church. Since Eliot demonstrates an altogether active relation to "those absurdities," since he attempts—quite as Orwell says—"to make them acceptable to himself" without ever yielding utterly, to the point of dumb submission, he should be given every benefit of the critical doubt. The critic will in such a case forebear from finding in the poet only what he expects to find in a man who wishes to submit absolutely to a doctrinal faith. Orwell writes of a man who "does not really *feel* his faith, but merely assents to it for complex reasons." But can it properly be said that a man "merely" assents for complex reasons? What can be more strenuously earned than an assent that is complexly motivated? If we saw in Eliot what Randall Jarrell once called "the familiar literary Christianity of *as if*, the belief in the necessity of belief," we should be tempted to conclude with Orwell that the poetry is no more than a calculated search for an available refuge. But Eliot is not the sort of man to be satisfied with anything that can be sought, and found, with so definite a sense of purpose as Orwell assigns him. The poetry bears witness to his misgiving, his tentativeness, his instinct for correction. Blackmur answers better to our sense of the *Quartets* when he speaks of Eliot's honesty, his willingness to let the poem be "a kind of provisional institution." For, Blackmur writes, there is in the *Quartets* an intimation of a faith so "full" that it cannot refuse to witness its "final predicament": that there may be, always (though *I* do not myself believe it), *another* path, *another* pattern of timeless moments; not an anarchy, not a damnation, but another pattern, another revelation."

For Blackmur, then, the content of Eliot's poem has everything to do with what it expresses and enacts, and little to do with the statement of a position on Christian doctrine. It is possible, in Blackmur's terms, to speak of an attitude that has, from the evidence of a given poem, hardened into a certainty, as if it issued from a doctrinal conviction. Such an attitude might then be said to shut down the poet's responsiveness to materials presented in his own poems, or to prevent him from entertaining thoughts that would in any way compromise his conviction. His poems would then move all too securely to realize a purpose determined in advance of composition, refusing to discover or acknowledge anything that might be sighted along the way. Hardy was the type of such a poet, Blackmur felt, and his still perfect essay on Hardy[6] attempts to prove that the poet succeeded—magnificently, occasionally—only in spite of predilections that would have done in a lesser artist. If it is

6. "The Shorter Poems of Thomas Hardy," in *Language as Gesture*, pp. 51–79.

easy to summarize the content of a Hardy poem, that is because it is usually nothing but a simple idea set conventionally in simple stanzas. The reader knows what the poem expects of him because he is asked only to register the controlling idea and to agree that life is sometimes as awful as it seems in Hardy's view of it. There is no way to resist the idea, no variety of options to move among, because the experience expressed in the poem is so totally encompassed by the idea. To resist is to resist the poem altogether, and that is all the discriminating reader can, in fact, bring himself to do. By dismissing the poem as willful, as an expression of a merely personal crotchet or obsession, we say, in effect, that the poet has insisted where he should have proposed, that he has mistaken an occasional insight for the totality of experience itself. It is impossible to discuss Hardy's poetry without getting into the content of his vision because the poems are so steadfastly reducible to the vision. And the vision disfigures the poems by making them tame and predictable.

There are, in Blackmur's view, several kinds of shorter poems by Hardy. Some appear to have been written solely for the purpose of stating, or proving, the poet's central ideas: that life is chance, that human beings cannot control their destinies, that it is best to look at human beings at their worst to know the truth about them. The clear majority of Hardy's poems belong in this category. Then there are the poems that, though they are in thrall to the same ideas, seem remarkably not to insist upon the ideas so strenuously, are content to work out a human drama in miniature and to let the pattern emerge as it will. Among these Blackmur finds a good number of what he calls "crossed fidelity" lyrics. The risk, even in the best of these poems, Blackmur identifies as the possibility "that the scaffold [the idea pattern] might become so much more important than the poetry as to replace it." Yeats's addiction to a private symbolism obviously exposed him to a similar risk, though he apparently resisted the seduction of ideas more consistently.

The best of Hardy's poems achieve what Blackmur calls *anonymity*. They constitute a very small proportion of the collected work and are the more remarkable for having so much in common with the many items that disappoint us. In simplicity of diction, straightforwardness of appeal, homely detail, and metrical flexibility, the better poems are very close to the others. They stand out, so Blackmur contends, because they have something to say that can be said without the author's saying it for himself. Their content is not an idea but an experience, not an obsession but the motive of a feeling. They are "anonymous," or nearly so, not because they pretend to an austere impersonality but because they do not appear to issue from a single-minded insistence that represented experience confirm everywhere the single formula the poet relies upon to do his thinking for him. Blackmur speaks of "the vanity of Hardy's adherence to his personal and crotchety obsessions" because those obsessions were merely personal. Hardy stuck with them because they were his, not because they enabled him to see things more clearly or to penetrate more deeply into the experiences he examined. He was content in most of his work to come up with the same insights and to rehearse the same situations, feeling that his overarching insight was bracing and terrible enough to warrant the repetition. What he did not consider was the fact that the situations were played over always in the same way and with no possibility of discovering another result. "Hardy's idea-patterns," Blackmur showed, "were not heuristic . . . , but were held rather as rigid frames to limit experience so far as possible and to substitute for what they could not enclose." The successful poems, by contrast, achieved anonymity precisely by permitting the material to speak for itself. There is in them no trace of eccentricity; no willfully idiosyncratic detail to announce that the poem belongs to one Hardy, Thomas; no insistence that the drama summarize what life is for all of us or confirm the poet's dire sense of circumstance pressing always to baffle our wishes. In achieving a "style reduced to anonymity," a style without visible pressure of the poet's shaping hand, Hardy strangely achieves a voice like no one else's, and yet like the voice of every other poet who could let his poem have its head. No wonder that Blackmur, looking for words to celebrate and account for Hardy's achievement, invokes the example of Yeats's "A Deep-Sworn Vow" and is tempted to conclude "that all Hardy had to do was to put it down."

The passages Blackmur selects to make his case serve nicely to persuade us that there was in Hardy a terrific need to be violated by ideas, a sense that life was an intolerable chaos without some explanatory formula to order it and make sense of it even in its randomness. And as the critic has no trouble in showing how routinely Hardy submitted to formula, he has great success in finding the poems that have no reason for being but the content of the represented experience. Here are two perfect examples, the first a passage from a lyric called "The Moth-Signal," the other a poem called "The Walk." In the first, we have the development of a simple domestic situation: "a husband reads, a moth burns in the candle flame, a wife waits and watches. After a light word or two, the wife goes out to look at the moon while the husband goes on with his reading." So Blackmur prepares us for what follows:

Outside the house a figure
    Came from the tumulus near,
And speedily waxed bigger,
    And clasped and called her Dear.

"I saw the pale-winged token
    You sent through the crack," sighed she.
"That moth is burnt and broken
    With which you lured out me."

"And were I as the moth is
    It might be better far
For one whose marriage troth is
    Shattered as potsherds are!"

In the next example, Blackmur presents one poem from a sequence of twenty-one Hardy wrote "after the death of his first wife, which appear under the motto: *Veteris Vestigia flammae.*" In his observations on the poem, Blackmur stresses the quality of impersonality and anonymity he so valued in the verse of his time.

The Walk

You did not walk with me
Of late to the hill-top tree
        By the gated ways,
        As in earlier days;
        You were weak and lame,
        So you never came,
And I went alone, and I did not mind,
Not thinking of you as left behind.

I walked up there to-day
Just in the former way;
    Surveyed around
    The familiar ground
    By myself again:
    What difference, then?
Only that underlying sense
Of the look of a room on returning thence.

Blackmur uses the stanzas from "The Moth-Signal" to show how Hardy's writing became "inexact" and awkward when he contrived to make his material say what it did not wish to say. How does the critic know the intentions inscribed in the material? By considering particular words in their given contexts, to be sure, but more importantly by considering the poem's "compositional strength, which is what is meant by inevitability." The imagery in the stanzas quoted is inexact, Blackmur concludes, because the poet has imposed his own willful order on the images to make them say what he wants them to. Had he permitted the "figure" outside the house to suggest what it had the power to suggest, he would not have needed the line on the "marriage troth . . . shattered as potsherds are!" Neither would he have required the heavy-handed irony of the poem's final stanza, in which the "figure" from the tumulus becomes "the Ancient Briton," and grinningly delivers himself of the observation that: "So, hearts are thwartly smitten/In these days as in mine!" Blackmur's central objection to all this—that it lacks inevitability—is borne out by the fact that we do not know by the end of the poem who precisely is the Ancient Briton and why anyone should care about the marital strife endured by this particular pair. He goes further, suggesting that, with a little reordering of the stanzas in question, the poem might make better sense, even if it could not be made more effective as an evocation of a condition of feeling. Inevitability the poem lacks because, for one thing, the images are imperfect; they do not quite say what they mean to say. And since they have no independent function, no life outside of their meaning, they blur what might otherwise be the poem's true direction. Most especially is this true of the burned moth.

And what is the poem's true direction? What does the figure outside the house have power to suggest? Blackmur wants the poem to conclude with the stanza preceding those he quoted, a stanza that, in its actual position, "merely kills time." In that stanza, the husband is described as "little heeding" as the wife goes out to meet her lover; more precisely, the husband is described as going on "With his mute and museful reading/In the annals of ages gone." By opting to put this material at the end of the poem, Blackmur recommends, in effect, that we read the entire thing as a poem about a man who is out of touch with "reality" and an unfortunate woman who is drawn to satisfy her senses more immediately. Fair enough. But he is right to say that the poem is only marginally improved in this way. It is possible to make better sense of the Ancient Briton by being forced to associate him with "the annals of ages gone," but it is still hard to see why that hoary figure should be invoked in a simple satire of circumstance like this. The poem's true direction, in fact, ought not to have been satirical at all, the target of the satire being too easy to support much in the way of indignation or even malicious jest. The poem is more truly about the woman's attraction to the figure outside than about the husband's attraction to the past. It would be easy, and a mistake, to read the poem as straight Lawrentian drama, but there is in fact an element of the Lawrentian darkness and brooding and violence that cannot be ignored. This element Blackmur doesn't get into because he doesn't feel compelled to discuss the poem's content *as such*, something he would do only if he felt the poem succeeded in bringing that content to life. Since it fails to realize its own project, even to organize its materials effectively, he cannot begin to worry over its "deeper" implications. That there are those implications we can certify by comparing the poem with an incident in *The Return of the Native* in which Eustacia and Wildeve meet outside through the agency of a moth, just as the lovers are brought together in the poem. In the novel, though, we get a meticulous development of the imagery so that it emerges gradually and persuasively as a body of workable symbols. This is true of the fire and of the Heath, for example. The Ancient Briton of the poem may hardly be said to operate with the force of the Heath as it broods over human frailty. And the fire into which the wife is tempted to fling herself is decidedly less fearsome than the fire to which the lovers in the novel are painfully, irresistibly attracted. By working out these contrasts, we see how utterly the poem fails to move us as it should, and how it fails to be what it should. If its true direction could not be realized, neither could the figure who steps out of the gloom to embrace the wife be made to suggest what he should. Who is he, after all, that he should have power so to draw the woman even as she moves about with "lost" eyes and a persisting desire to be done with a life that is "broken" and full of guilt? Hardy's inability, or unwillingness, to motivate the woman adequately or to make of the lover more than a shadowy presence reflects a failure to engage the real possibilities inherent in his own dramatic materials.

John Crowe Ransom could, in his work on Hardy,[7] concern himself for a brief while with effects, with workmanship, and with tone as an element of style. But he could announce securely that, in dealing with such a writer, we come quickly, inevitably, "to the meaning, which is our major preoccupation, and Hardy's." And he could go on to interpret the simplest Hardy poems, quite in the spirit of E. D. Hirsch's "interpreter," who looks for "textual meaning, in and for itself." The assumption at work is that any reader who respects or loves Hardy's poems will be interested in his "views," and that these views can be isolated and evaluated as views. Ransom had no appetite for extended versions of such interpretative procedures, but he did clearly feel that Hardy's poetry could be discussed as the working out of particular views and theological assumptions. Blackmur, on the other hand, is said—by Schwartz and others—to be uninterested in views and to concern himself with content only under protest. Even poems that had something to say and managed to say that something perfectly would be evaluated not as representations of a content but as poems, art objects designed to give pleasure and to certify certain aesthetic possibilities. Blackmur's critics might have wished to adduce his treatment of "The Walk" as a case in point. Here was a poem the critic could admire without reservation. What had he to say of it, beyond that? Only that, in the poem, "all that was personal—the private drive, the private grief—is cut away and the impersonal is left bare, an old monument, mutilated or

7. See his introduction to *Selected Poems of Thomas Hardy* (New York: Macmillan, Inc., 1961).

weathered as you like to call it, of that face which the personal only hides." What does this amount to? If interpretation is a search for textual meaning, in and for itself, Blackmur's comments do not constitute an interpretation. But does the poem require an interpretation? It seems not to make any unusual demands. Nothing is gained by reflecting, with one recent academic interpreter, that " 'the look of a room on returning thence' after Emma's death has intimations of the significance of the lacking figure." Of course it does, but who would fail to see this? Blackmur's observation is ever so much subtler. It is also more helpful in getting at the true content of the poem, which is not the horror of death or the misery of the bereaved. For Blackmur, what matters is not simply that Hardy wrote a great poem, but that he bore witness to a great truth by thinking poetically. To think poetically is to know that the personal motive, the initiating circumstance or feeling must be expressed *as the form* of the motive or feeling. That form can only be gestured at, suggested, by allowing the chosen situation to unfold. Any poet's attempt to "read" the situation for the reader, to install the meaning deliberately, is bound to violate the form of the emotion that arises naturally from contemplation of and submission to the relevant particulars. In "The Walk," the "face which the personal only hides" is the face at once of true suffering and of release from suffering in the accession of understanding and affection the poem enables. The great truth Hardy witnesses, creates, is the truth of experience raised to an impersonality in which all that is peculiar to poet or personae is subsumed by something larger and more permanent. The poem enacts a possibility in which the poet surpasses himself by working through the content of his experience only to leave it behind.

But see how inadequate are the various statements of Hardy's content or meaning or truth that we have generated to "improve upon" Blackmur's resonant formulation. What these statements lack, in fact, is just the fine economy of Blackmur's observation, the audacious image of the monument revealed to the critic in the opening out of Hardy's poem. Those more skeptical of Blackmur's gift than I believe that he resorted so often to poetic images—in his critical prose—to cover over large gaps in his knowledge and to prevent him from having to work out his impressions more carefully. This seems to me insupportable. Anyone who has seen him "re-write" a Hardy poem by shuffling the stanzas or altering key words will know that he was a scrupulous reader and commentator. The issue here is not, cannot be, Blackmur's seriousness, but the ability of his method to take on meaning, what ordinarily passes for content in a poem. And it is my feeling that, though he did not aim to uncover textual meanings in the spirit of an academic interpreter, he had an eye for what was essential and knew how to suggest, at least, what would be most important to the reader of a contemporary poem. Perhaps he avoided the muddle most of us get stuck in when we talk about the "truth" of a poem only because he stayed away from the "truth" more resolutely than other critics. But there is no denying that he suggested more about the concerns, the main thrust of a poem, in a sentence or two than the rest of us are likely to manage in several heavy-breathing paragraphs. For truth-content he preferred what he called "access of being" and intended thereby to argue that if poetry was not a supreme fiction it could not have a content worth uncovering. What was the supreme fiction? It was the embodiment of our collective desire "to conceive, to imagine, to make a supreme being, . . . to discover and objectify a sense of such a being." Such a being, Blackmur went on to say in his short essay on "Wallace Stevens: An Abstraction Blooded,"[8] had about it an aspect of abstraction; also, it was subject to change and could give pleasure. Was Hardy's poem "The Walk" a supreme fiction in Blackmur's view of it? It was, in the degree that it seemed to him sufficient, its own reason for being. It could invite the participation of readers without asking them to see in it a symptom of something external to it. And it could, finally, invite a response that was reverent without compromising anyone's desire to account for the poem's unusual power and clarity. The "access of being" it enabled was a content in the sense that we speak of a final content in any poem, a content that is more than the sum of the several views or inspirations that may have figured in the poem's evolution. To speak of "That face which the personal only hides," as Blackmur does in his lines on "The Walk," is to speak of a content that is not an idea about something but a fact in itself. We are moved by it because it is an emblem of creation, because, as Blackmur says in

8. In *Language as Gesture,* pp. 250–54.

another of his short pieces on Stevens, "it is part of the regular everlasting job of making over again the absolute content of sensibility with which we get on, or with which we acknowledge our failures to do so."[9]

Blackmur's insistence on "the absolute content of sensibility" was for him the only way of bearing witness to content in poetry. For poetry was the creation of sensibility, the raising of sensibility to the status of fact. Stevens's work might get lost in a fire, Blackmur said, but it would survive all the same—at least "in the work that followed it." Like Hardy's, "his work is part of the history of poetry, which, like orthodoxy, exists whether anyone knows it or not." Now this may be taken as an evasion of the entire question of content in poetry. We all know that poems do have something to say, or that many poems do. And we know that, if poems exist as facts in the world, as enactments of sensibility we acknowledge whether we wish to or not, they exist also as attitudes or assumptions or "views." Do we not, and with a sense of knowing what we are doing, distinguish Ezra Pound's attitudes toward democracy from, say, Robert Frost's? And is it not possible to say, after inspecting the relevant poems, what W. H. Auden thought about Freudian psychoanalysis? If poems enable this kind of knowledge, it might be said, they must be taken to have a content that is different from the creation of sensibility. Poems may be supreme fictions, but they often manifest a content that is less than the final content Blackmur sought to identify. It matters, in Pound's *Cantos*, that Pound indulged particular attitudes toward Jews, and it is foolish to pretend that Auden's views of politics did not affect the shape of whatever final content he achieved.

No one will object, at this point, if I say that Blackmur understood all of this quite as well as anyone else. We have seen that, for Blackmur, ideas could be as interesting as they were for another sort of critic entirely. And he showed, in his later work especially, that politics and cultural institutions could be quite as absorbing to the literary mind as poems or stories. We go on with the question of content here because it is so central to our concern with poetical thinking. The content Blackmur could not honor was a

9. "On Herbert Read and Wallace Stevens," in *Language as Gesture*, pp. 255–59.

content that was nothing but a sentiment, an attitude or an idea. He was ready to accept that certain ideas were more attractive than others, or that a particular attitude would readily serve the gifts of a particular poet. But in themselves these ideas or attitudes were not the facts that could inspire a final sympathy or allegiance. Eliot's mind was a fact in the more final sense, his better poems an enactment of his sensibility that would stand, permanently, as an emblem of a certain kind of possibility realized. Call it the possibility of a mind divided against itself but working strenuously all the same at a wholeness it associated with utter singleness of purpose. Call it something else. It is not—that mind, those poems—a conviction that only in Christ may we be saved. It is not—in the case of Pound—the view that Jews are the bane of western civilization and must be eradicated if conditions are to improve. Blackmur insisted on another view of content because he wanted to encourage the conception of poetry as mind thinking, working, changing—creating and unmaking all at once. "Poetry *thinks* by giving the actual experience—the *make-believe*—of thought." This he wrote in trying to get at what, in Stevens, could move us, even where the issue of the thought was relatively trivial. Most important, he wished to say, the poem "does not convert thought into poetry, except at the expense of both." And so, it may be said, the poem may not be translated back into mere thought or, worse yet, mere thoughts, if it is to remain for us a wonder, a final fact. Our way of talking—or of refusing certain temptations to talk—about the poem's content is the measure of our ability to think poetically. For Blackmur, that was the essential measure.

IV. EXPRESSIVE FORM, AND OTHER FALLACIES

The critic Gerald Graff has lately stimulated discussion of New Criticism as an approach to texts that has nothing at all to do with methodological orthodoxy. In fact, he has shown, a man like Blackmur assigned himself goals that could not have been undertaken by, say, I. A. Richards or Allen Tate. These critics, and the others familiarly associated with them, did have at least one important thing in common, though. They resisted, in Graff's terms, "the scientific reduction of literature to technical subtleties." That they have been accused—by latter-day structuralists especially—of bringing literary texts to their knees, of insisting upon the one-dimensional, objective content of poems, indicates only how far from the truth people can stray in seeking to justify their own avowedly "radical" procedures. "It is odd," Graff notes, "that the New Critics should be denounced for their arid scientific empiricism, since this was one of the chief cultural ills which the New Critics themselves sought to combat. . . . The methodology of 'close reading' was an attempt not to imitate science but to refute its devaluation of literature: by demonstrating the rich complexity of meaning within even the simplest poem, the New Critic proved . . . that literature had to be taken seriously as a rival mode of cognitive knowledge."[1] In fact, we have seen, it was not so much the meaning of poetry conceived as a tissue of complex statements that the New Critic was after; Blackmur at least—and Eliot too—was interested less in cognitive knowledge than in ways of knowing, less in thoughts than in thinking. If texts were to be read closely, they could be expected to yield, not certainties or principles, but a point of view. Texts that mistook their own points of view for the truth were not on that account to be dismissed, but they were to be met with skepticism and a repertoire of alternative propositions. Critics who sought in texts nothing but confirmation of their own ideas would necessarily be read out of the New Critical fraternity—though Blackmur cared little for rites of

1. See Gerald Graff's *Literature against Itself* (Illinois: University of Chicago Press, 1979).

66

excommunication—and those who were attached mainly to formal niceties would never attract much of a following.

Nothing could be further from arid scientific empiricism than Blackmur's "close reading" of the modernist poets. Nor do many of the essays resemble what most of us take to be a close reading of a text. Though there is a concern for particular words and images, mostly the critic is concerned to elaborate an argument, to formulate in his own terms what the poet thinks he is doing and what in fact he does. We call these expository formulations "an argument" because they are proposed, frankly, as a version of the poet's project, a project susceptible at once to the critic's sympathy and corrective evaluation. There is, of course, some presumption of objectivity: Blackmur would not for a moment allow that he had simply made up his version of the poetry, attributing to this writer or that only those qualities the critic wished to dispute or support. But he does feel, clearly, that what he has to say is far from self-evident and needs to be represented with a strenuousness of critical appeal that is closer to argument than to straightforward laying out of evidence. Randall Jarrell, by contrast, felt that what he had to say about Moore and Frost and some of the others could be demonstrated largely by selecting appropriate passages from the relevant texts and by quoting them at length. In his essays on Lowell and Auden, he was less confident that this would do and was apparently more content to use Blackmur as a model. In any case, in neither poet-critic does close reading ever amount to an orderly moving through the poem, as if all one had to do was to fasten on things in sequence, count meters, and look up difficult words in order to arrive at an acceptable reading. Blackmur's readings are strenuous and argumentative not because he had a negative approach to the work of his contemporaries—whatever that means—but because engagement with the thought of others is always and properly a strenuous business. The readings are "close" only in the sense that the critic tries to account for the essential project without ignoring aspects of the work that refuse to submit to his account. There is no pretense of exhaustively accounting for everything, though some of the other New Critics— like Cleanth Brooks—may have felt it was possible to say as much as the given poem would allow.

Blackmur, then, could talk about a particular "fallacy"

in a poem or in an entire body of work without intending thereby to suggest that he had uttered the last word on the subject. He spoke with authority because he felt he had subjected the poems to the test of his own sympathy. Those that failed, ultimately, to satisfy him were deficient primarily in the sense that they had not been adequate to what was best in their authors. To be sure, some of the work he was asked to review hardly merited extended appraisal, and he often dismissed a new volume in a paragraph or two. But these were not the critical performances we remember. Most often he wrote about authors who had some real ability and who, for one reason or another, were content to do only what came naturally to them. Carl Sandburg was such a poet, and because he is now almost entirely ignored by literary professionals, it is instructive to recall the terms in which Blackmur put him, as it were, in his place.[2] It was no outright dismissal Blackmur sought to fashion, but a brief, determinedly limiting appraisal that would be reinforced by the critic's related treatment of other, more demanding writers. It might have been tempting to deny that Sandburg had any place at all in modern poetry, but he'd had his supporters, and it seemed clearly necessary to try to submit, provisionally, to his spell. Something "saves the work and makes it have almost the value of poetry," Blackmur was forced to conclude. What carries it as far as it goes, he decided, was "the freshness of the surface of what he sees" so that, for Sandburg's reader, there would be "a momentary sense of relation between the elements of perception." The poem concluded, the reader's attention even temporarily distracted, the experience of the thing would seem—and rightly—beyond recovery.

This might not have seemed self-evident to everyone, but it was clear to Blackmur that even extended quotation would not help to persuade those who would not be moved by his argument. So much was certain: Sandburg, as a poet, had no point of view. An occasional stray sentiment, perhaps, but no elaborated angle of vision. There were, to be sure, the materials of a vision: the persons, events, landscapes out of which other writers would make something

2. See "The Composition in Nine Poets 1937" collected in *The Expense of Greatness* (New York: Arrow Editions, 1940; reprint ed., Gloucester, Mass.: Peter Smith, 1958).

we could take hold of. But for Sandburg there was no need to make something when the materials were themselves rich and had shapes of their own. The poetry, Blackmur argued, "sprawls dangerously on the original level of its subject matter." It is, he went on, a representation of "experience at that level where it is taken to be its own expression." The assumption underlying this poetry was that "the act of expression creates its own adequate form." It made room but fitfully, and then "only by accident," for the kind of controlling intelligence we recognize in the creations of writers who participate more responsibly in the unfolding of their material.

It didn't matter whether or not Sandburg actually found or made up what he put down on paper and passed off as poetry. What mattered was that the poems didn't take hold and couldn't—as no more than their manifest subject matter—be expected to. Blackmur didn't object to the subject matter itself, or think it in any way inappropriate for the kinds of things a Sandburg might have done with it. He objected to a poetry that was, he said, "innately beyond control," that was, in other words, resistant to the significance that comes from a shaping vision and a point of view. Is it a shaping vision that puts together Abe Lincoln, Ulysses Grant, and Pocahontas in the poem "Cool Tombs" that used so often to grace anthologies of American verse?

> When Abraham Lincoln was shoveled into the tombs, he forgot the copperheads and the assassin . . . in the dust, in the cool tombs.
>
> And Ulysses Grant lost all thought of con men and Wall Street, cash and collateral turned ashes . . . in the dust, in the cool tombs.
>
> Pocahontas' body, lovely as a poplar, sweet as a red haw in November or a pawpaw in May, did she wonder? does she remember? . . . in the dust, in the cool tombs?
>
> Take any streetful of people buying clothes and groceries, cheering a hero or throwing confetti and blowing tin horns . . . tell me if the lovers are losers . . . tell me if any get more than the lovers . . . in the dust . . . in the cool tombs.

Of such a poem Blackmur would surely have said what

he thought of Sandburg in general: that it depends on "the fallacy of expressive form."[3] "Cool Tombs" may demonstrate a certain coherence, may even contain the shadow of a sentiment. But it achieves, on the whole, only a "momentary sense of relation between the elements of perception." What are the elements? There are the figures themselves, and there are the incidents or characteristics typically associated with them. The incidents do not, however, define the figures or sharpen our perception of them in a way that would make any reader grateful to Sandburg. Even where the details are marginally eccentric—the "people . . . blowing tin horns," Grant's "cash and collateral turned ashes"—they do not rise much above the level of cliché. Blackmur's more radical criticism, though, is that, whatever the freshness or triteness of any particular locution or detail, Sandburg's poems do not elaborate or proceed from a point of view. In "Cool Tombs," we may say, though Lincoln is to Grant as Grant is to Pocahontas as all are to "any streetful of people," no distinctive human possibility is brought to our awareness in a way that would make us see the human prospect more clearly than we had before. The particulars of the poem have only "a momentary sense of relation" because there is no underlying connection between them, no shaping vision that makes them seem *necessarily* to belong together. It is not possible that the reader of the poem will henceforth think always of Grant when he thinks of Lincoln, or of the lovely Indian princess when he thinks of ordinary persons moving toward the cool tombs. The prospect of death itself is not a sufficiently distinctive point of view to unify otherwise disparate particulars and to raise to significance what is in the poem a vague sentiment of regret over all that passes. The poem is "innately beyond control" in the sense that the mere mention of "dust" and "cool tombs" in each of the four stanzas cannot say enough about the other particulars to make us feel that the poet has brought them into meaningful focus. Nor can the refrain words help us to understand why these particulars, these persons and their fates, were better suited to illuminating the poet's theme than others he might have chosen.

3. Blackmur never singled out "Cool Tombs" for analysis, but the poem yields nicely to his argument.

To say of "Cool Tombs" that it is no more than its "manifest subject matter," as Blackmur so often complained of Sandburg and of other poets, is to say that the subject is not allowed the significance it might have earned. The poet has not thought through his material with a view toward making it enter into pointed relation with his own insistent needs and specific insights. He has relied upon the material to be its own sufficient reason for being, thus falling prey, as Blackmur has it, to the fallacy of expressive form. This fallacy—"the most common of our time," Blackmur says— "consists in the belief that the act of expression creates its own adequate form." Thus, in "Cool Tombs," the act of expression may be said to be the juxtaposition, in four stanzas, of the figures of Lincoln, Grant, Pocahontas, and the people with some hope that these can heighten our apprehension of the end that awaits each of us. The details drawn "from life" are to interest us not in themselves or for anything they may have to tell us of actual historical figures but as vague indications of all that is swept from sight as the years pass. A form more adequate to the assembled materials would make us feel that they had been subjected to the poet's scrutiny, not as occasions for the expression of a sentiment that obviously existed before them but as the necessary conditions of that sentiment.

Blackmur has more to say of this in the famous essay on Lawrence.[4] There he writes of the poet as "an incomplete, uncomposed mind: a mind without defenses against the material with which it builds and therefore at every point of stress horribly succumbing to it." The emphasis falls, not as in the Sandburg review, on the absence of a controlling intelligence but on the relation between feeling and its expression in verse. With Sandburg the problem had seemed constitutive: since the poet's private apprehension of the world was in no way an affair of genius, he was positively required to elaborate usable forms to fill out and shape his meanings. Lawrence, on the other hand, saw things with so ferocious and unsettling an intensity that he managed often to move his readers to wonder even without bothering to discover forms adequate to the issues. If Lawrence succumbed to his material, he at least managed so to invest the

4. "D. H. Lawrence and Expressive Form," in *Language as Gesture* (New York: Harcourt, Brace and Co., 1952), pp. 286–300.

material with feeling that no reader would fail to sense the urgency. Blackmur could direct at Lawrence a devastating critique without, for a moment, forgetting that he had in hand works of undeniable genius. He detested the view— "the pretension," he called it—"that the radical imperfection of poetry is a fundamental virtue." This view, stated in the Preface to Lawrence's *Collected Poems,* and subsequently taken up by all manner of poets in the United States especially, is a perfect complement to the notion that immediacy is all that matters in poetry. Lawrence so absorbed Blackmur's attention because he had all the natural gifts of a great writer but had managed to compromise those gifts by insisting upon the sufficiency of his own intuition. Blackmur might have discussed this as a failure of character in Lawrence, and there are suggestions in his essay that he was tempted to do so. But he decided for the most part to discuss the problem as a failure of technique, of art. No account of the poetry would be convincing without some mention of the hysterical dimension in Lawrence, the obsessional component in his thought. But in the end, it was not as a neurotic, as a "mental case" that he represented himself to us. He was a poet who, with the greatest sincerity and relentless conviction, betrayed his art.

To arrive at this conclusion, Blackmur had only to read through the poems and to put to them more or less ordinary questions: What did they know? What did they invite a reader to believe and to feel? Did they present a vision that was accessible, or did the vision seem too entirely a function of the poet's private obsessions? There was no doubt that the critic had done a "close reading" of the poems, but he did not think it necessary to take the reader by the hand and recapitulate his own movement from line to line. Very few of Lawrence's poems are referred to by name, and he quotes only twenty-five lines of verse in an essay of approximately six thousand words. No doubt, having determined as usual not to concentrate too much on the prose-content of Lawrence's verse, he was subject to the usual complaints: that he was indifferent to content and that he reduced poems to scientific subtleties. The fact that he isolated few individual words or images in the essay would not exempt him from the charge that there was nothing but hair-splitting in this piece as in the others.

Lawrence seemed to Blackmur to have written at least a

handful of arresting poems in spite of his usual practice. The poet had the obvious advantage of a subject matter that was, on the face of it, acceptable to most readers. "As it happens," Blackmur wrote, "Lawrence's obsessions ran to sex, death, the isolation of the personality, and the attempt at mystical fusion. Had he run rather to claustrophobia, fetish-worship, or some of the more obscure forms of human cowardice, his method of expression would have been less satisfactory." Since the poet did not fully master his obsessions in his verse, since the insistent expression of those obsessions is very much what the poems are about, it was necessary for him to be moved by obsessions that were neither disgusting nor altogether depressing to others. He succeeded in some of his poems because the issues he raised were interesting to others and because his obsession with them was expressed in plain language. Too often he succumbed to what Blackmur calls "fake 'poetic' language" (see "Lift looks of shocked and momentous emotion" in "After the Opera") or "plain empty verbiage" (of the kind that disfigures even an impressive poem like "The Song of a Man Who Has Come Through"). Occasionally he relied upon a language utterly "commonplace for everything except its intensity." In those instances, Blackmur judged, he avoided "violating the communicative residue of his words," so that "so much of his intention is available to the reader as is possible in work that has not been submitted to the completing persuasiveness of a genuine form."

Blackmur's argument is convincing, but it would seem to me rather more instructive if it emerged from just the sort of *represented* close reading his detractors deplore. Blackmur tells us what the poems know, and he is clear at least on what they make him feel. But does the argument do justice to all of Lawrence's better poems? The critic eludes some potential antagonists by excluding from rigorous consideration early poems like "Lightning" and "Turned down," on the grounds that they too strongly resemble the poems of Hardy, particularly items in the *Satires of Circumstance*. But this leaves poems like "Snake," "The Ship of Death," even the overrated "Bavarian Gentians" to consider. Blackmur makes a special place in his essay—as in his affections—for a less ambitious poem called "Corot," claiming that there "Lawrence provided himself, for once, with a principle of objective form." What Lawrence needed, apparently, was

"The constant presence of an external reference"—in this poem, the figure of the painter himself and of the landscape imagery he created—to temper his predilection for vague, dimly suggestive language and "inconsistent meters." But is it not the case that, in a number of poems, Lawrence managed to create a sufficient form without having to rely upon an external reference? No one will pretend that Lawrence was a master of forms like Eliot or Pound; that is not the issue. He did write moving and successful poems that are neither derivative nor simple. Consider only the nine lines of Section II in "The Ship of Death":

> Have you built your ship of death, O have you?
> O build your ship of death, for you will need it.
>
> The grim frost is at hand, when the apples will fall
> thick, almost thundrous, on the hardened earth.
>
> And death is on the air like a smell of ashes!
> Ah! can't you smell it?
>
> And in the bruised body, the frightened soul
> finds itself shrinking, wincing from the cold
> that blows upon it through the orifices.

The words in this poem may indeed be said to be commonplace, but it is not merely the intensity of utterance that makes them special. In fact, for all the prophetic intimation in the lines, the intensity is hardly the intensity of hysteria. The words command our attention because they are made to operate in ways that are unusual. Is this not the case with many great poets? Not all are inclined to the verbal opulence or variety of a Stevens or a Keats. The word *thundrous* is commonplace, or nearly so, but it works so well for Lawrence because it is rarely used to describe the "thick" falling of apples "on the hardened earth." And though we all of us know about "orifices," we don't ordinarily hear of the soul "wincing from the cold" blowing through them. Such combinations, precisely in their unfamiliarity, will often seem awkward or merely clever in the poems of most writers. But Lawrence's words seem earnest and true.

Is there, in "The Ship of Death," any trace of the fallacy that, in Blackmur's view, so compromises the poems? Is the poem "a plea, really, for the reader to do the work the poet failed to do," to "complete" that for which Lawrence provided only "the expressive outlines"? In some of the parts, no doubt, Blackmur's contention seems irresistible. Particularly when the poet gestures at the "coming back to life/out of oblivion" in Parts IX and X he seems to invite the reader to believe him without furnishing for the reader any cause to warrant the belief. The gesture is not so much halfhearted as willful and insubstantial. The colorings of hope, the "flash of yellow" and "of rose" that contradict "the deathly ashy grey" are alright in themselves, but more would seem required to turn the tide of a poem that has run on so sombrely for several pages. One doesn't reject the poem at last, but one does feel that Lawrence has had less to say about the reemergence into life than the poem requires. One accepts the resolution, as it were, only by taking up the slender suggestive threads Lawrence has left about and fashioning for oneself the completion Lawrence means to have achieved in the medium of the poem. The reader's responsibility here goes beyond participation. It is something closer to assistance that Lawrence invites, and the thought to which he bears witness is, therefore, more shadowy and unrealized than he imagines.

Blackmur did not intend to say, in his discussion of Lawrence, that the poems were weak because of the absence of this quality or that. They were less than they might have been because they were based upon an "operative principle" Blackmur discovered in the poems he admired. This principle, "that the chaos of private experience cannot be known or understood until it is projected and ordered in a form external to the consciousness that entertained it in flux," might be violated or discounted in one or another instance, but it could not be routinely ignored. Lawrence had great gifts, to be sure, but he had also an unfortunate tendency to believe that chaos was valuable in itself and needed only to be projected as it appeared to the inspired poet to modify consciousness and alter behavior. His diagnosis of a diseased civilization was that it could be restored to health only by being forced to confront the fact of negation. That negation he bodied forth as chaos and death, believing that those who were willing to be scattered, "torn," might conceivably become "whole again," as he promised in his tortoise poems.[5] Blackmur argued that "the

5. "Tortoise Shell" and "Tortoise Shout" in *Birds, Beasts, and Flowers* (London: Jonathan Cape, 1923).

great mystics saw no more profoundly than Lawrence through the disorder of life to their ultimate vision, but they saw within the terms of an orderly insight." The critic's call for a form external to the initiating poetic consciousness may seem unduly straitening and academic, but it is no more repressive really than the idea of an objective correlative promoted by Eliot in the same period. And what is this "form"? Blackmur once called it "the limiting principle by which a thing becomes itself." That helps. He also got at it in the title essay of *Language as Gesture*. Distinguishing between a bad and a good church spire, he saw that "bad spires weigh a church down and are an affair of carpentry . . . A good spire," on the other hand, "is weightless, springing, an arrow aimed at the Almighty, carrying, in its gesture, the whole church with it. Though it may have been as much made out of formula as the bad spire, it differs in that the formula has somehow seized enough life to become form again; which is one way of saying what gesture does in art—it is what happens to a form when it becomes identical with its subject."

So the form in a successful work may be said to become "identical" with its subject. So "we feel," Blackmur concludes, "that pillars are mighty, that a bridge spans or leaps, that a dome covers us, or a crypt appalls us." The reader will note, in these examples, that Blackmur relies upon formal identities that are in general less problematic than anything proposed in poems or novels. It is possible to speak of tautology in a certain kind of poem without implying that there is but one way of formulating the tautology. The words in a poem may seem perfectly inevitable, their order determined by a vision that unfolds inexorably. But we know that even in such a poem identity is not so easy to define. We may seek to define the form of the poem by locating an organizing principle—a metaphor, an emotion, an ideological abstraction—or a poetic convention, but rarely will we conclude that the form has become identical with its subject. The difficulty will have much to do with our inability to say what exactly is the subject. With Lawrence we may speak of death, rebirth, mystical communion of souls, and so on, without feeling that we have got at the heart of the thing. Blackmur would no doubt counsel us, at a certain point in our exertions, to worry less about getting it right in words of our own, to simply acknowledge the rightness the poem had managed somehow to make self-evident.

Perhaps that is the only advice we should accept, finally, though it doesn't seem to me that Blackmur was as easy with it as he sometimes liked us to believe. In any case, in light of Blackmur's strenuous objections to expressive form and his insistence upon alternative forms, it should be possible to take a Lawrence poem and to articulate, precisely, the relevant discriminations. Bearing in mind Blackmur's exemplary spires, pillars, bridges, domes, and crypts, let us consider the following lines from Lawrence's "Kangaroo":[6]

> Still she watches with eternal, cocked wistfulness!
> How full her eyes are, like the full, fathomless, shining
>   eyes of an Australian black-boy
> Who has been lost so many centuries on the margins of
>   existence!
> She watches with insatiable wistfulness.
> Untold centuries of watching for something to come,
> For a new signal from life, in that silent lost land of the
> South.
>
> Where nothing bites but insects and snakes and the sun,
>   small life.
> Where no bull roared, no cow ever lowed, no stag cried, no
>   leopard screeched, no lion coughed, no dog barked.
> But all was silent save for parrots occasionally, in the
>   haunted blue bush.
>
> Wistfully watching, with wonderful liquid eyes.
> And all her weight, all her blood, dripping sack-wise
>   down towards the earth's centre,
> And the live little-one taking in its paw at the door
>   of her belly.
>
> Leap then, and come down on the line that draws to the
>   earth's deep, heavy centre.

Blackmur didn't cite this poem in his essay. He should have, for it has in many ways an "answer" to his characteristic objections without altogether refuting them. The poem has no conventional form if by form we mean a shape or a rhyme scheme. It sometimes seems to run on a bit longer in one direction than it should, as in the sentence beginning

6. The poem appeared originally in *Birds, Beasts, and Flowers.*

with: "where no bull roared, no cow . . . "Blackmur would have to object to the way the poet leads us, installing in the verse the "prose" interpretation of the object he wishes to evoke, as in "lost so many centuries on the margins of existence!" He would object also to the heavy, overly self-conscious alliterations, as in "Wistfully watching, with wonderful . . . " The poem is clumsy almost, one might say, by intention. It expresses the speaker's *spontaneous* sentiment of affinity as he appropriates the creature to his vision of life. He wants to see it as it is, to give it its due, but he doesn't for a moment consider that to do so he must create a form external to his consciousness of it. It is what it is because the poet sees it in a way that is consistent with his own characteristic vision. Without that vision, the creature would be inert, an object among other lifeless, and, therefore, worthless things. So Lawrence would put the case.

Is there a form in the poem—is the poem itself a form—that may be said to become identical with its subject? If by subject we mean here *kangaroo,* the answer may be yes. One critic, in a brief but helpful book on Lawrence,[7] argues that "the form of the poem is exactly right." I don't know that I would go so far, or that it is possible to know that any poem so obviously flawed is "exactly right." But Anthony Beal nicely states that "No one else has observed animals in quite this way—with tenderness, penetration and a slangy sort of *camaraderie*—yet with never a hint of sentimentality." Of the animal poems generally he goes on to say that "there is something childlike . . . in the ease and lack of self-consciousness with which Lawrence perceives." The suggestion, of course, is that these childlike qualities are appropriate to poems about animals, and that the poem does therefore find a form, a voice that is somehow identical with its subject. The form may have originated in a formula (animal innocence equals childlike lack of self-consciousness), but the poem is so far from seeming a formula, so far from appealing to us as a piece of meticulous crafting or contrivance, that we yield to it quite easily. If the form doesn't quite have the inevitability of the leaping bridge or the covering dome, it does have a freshness we presumably associate with so peculiar a creature observed in its remote habitat. Despite Lawrence's heavy-breathing opening

7. Anthony Beal, *D. H. Lawrence* (New York: Grove Press, 1961).

stresses on the relative isolation and wistfulness of the thing, the poem does impress upon us the strangely emblematic qualities of a life even so unusual as the kangaroo's.

This is mostly obvious stuff, to be sure, but it is instructive to remind oneself of how nicely some of Blackmur's poetic principles may "fit" the better poems even of lesser masters like Lawrence. Blackmur did not, it may be, grant to Lawrence as poet all he deserved. The Lawrence essay stands, however, as a supreme probing of the question of form and an example of corrective criticism that focuses not on single words and images but on the poet's characteristic habits of thought. We can make good use of "Kangaroo"—apart from the sheer pleasure we take in it—by thinking of it as Blackmur would have instructed. And our pleasure is at once enhanced and tempered by bringing to bear the reservations he proposed as a necessary dimension of critical—which is to say, thoughtful—reading. "The fallacy of expressive form" is as close as we are likely to come to a statement of the central issue in Lawrence.

Are there other comparable fallacies Blackmur "exposed" in the poetry of the modernist period? Each of the main essays identifies one fallacy at least, or a constitutive problem, and some of the formulations have rightly come to be considered "unanswerable," as Helen Vendler recently noted in recalling the Cummings study.[8] With the essays themselves less present to us than many readers expected fifteen or twenty years ago, it may be useful in concluding this essay to isolate some of the classic formulations. In each will be seen Blackmur's capacity to read closely without losing sight of the poem as a process of thought realized, or betrayed.

1. "The Method of Marianne Moore":[9] Blackmur admired Moore, and without the sort of ambivalence he felt for poets like Crane or Lawrence. His essay is devoted almost entirely to a description of the things she did well, of a typical poem's "courtesy and aloofness of formal grace," of its ability to capture objects by setting them apart and polishing them scrupulously. There are even comparisons with

8. See Helen Vendler's "Poet's Gallery," *New York Review of Books,* 7 February 1980.
9. In *Language as Gesture,* pp. 260–85.

Keats, and with Eliot, with no accompanying sense that Moore is being placed in the company of her superiors. Her procedures are said to be perfectly geared to accomplishing the things she imagined for them. The critic even abandons his usual predilection for poetry-as-tautology so as to make room in his canon for Moore: "there is no meeting Miss Moore face to face in the forest of her poems and saying this is she, this is what she means and is." We may expect to meet her and to encompass her in this way, but shall be disappointed if we persist in the expectation. There is nothing wrong, so Blackmur argues, with a poetry that puts things together not so much to know them as to "produce a new relation" and to follow out the emotion produced by observing those things in momentary contiguity. So what if the emotions thereby produced are neither "general" nor "expansive"—as they are in Keats—but "special and specific"? Moore managed wonderfully to agitate her poetic surfaces and to produce some corresponding agitation in her readers. Those readers may not have been shaken to their roots, but they were stimulated to keep up with the ingenuities of her phrasing and the spare music of her "expedient forms."

What, then, may one conclude about Moore? Not that the poetry was itself built upon a fallacy or might have been better than it was. It was a mistake, though, to think of it as major poetry simply because it worked as well as anyone had a right to expect. Moore knew her limitations—temperamental mostly—and moved at ease within them, never putting undue strain upon the forms she contrived. Blackmur couldn't bring himself to deplore those limitations, or Moore's refusal to press against them. But one may be permitted to wonder what he meant when, near the end of his essay, he spoke of the poem "Marriage" as "an excellent poem," and went on to say: It is "never conceived with either love or lust, but with something else, perhaps no less valuable, but certainly, in a profound sense, less complete." To say that the poem is, "in a profound sense," concerned with something "less complete" than the given materials would seem to recommend, ought to amount to a judgment of insufficiency. And that is what it seems to me. Nor is Blackmur's response pinned to one poem alone. "There is no sex anywhere in her poetry," he observes, and goes on to speak of it as in part "an expression of cultivated distaste." To be sure, the poetry is all of a piece, knows better than to allow in "obviously stirring" materials that would violate the norms, which are "quiet and conversational." But something is lacking, Blackmur feels: though we have not the right to complain or chastize, we know that with Moore we are in the presence of something narrow and remote. The critic's closing ploy—an attempt to place her in a gallery of nineteenth-century Americans like James and Dickinson, masters of avoidance all—fails to convince us that he has satisfactorily put to rest his own barely articulated misgivings.

For sample passages expressing Blackmur's hesitant misgiving, we cannot do better than the following. No determinate fallacy is "exposed," but a habit of thought is authoritatively evaluated.

> [Her method] is integral to the degree that, with her sensibility being what it is, it imposes limits more profoundly than it liberates poetic energy. And here is one reason—for those who like reasons—for the astonishing fact that none of Miss Moore's poems attempt to be major poetry, why she is content with smallness in fact so long as it suggests the great by implication. Major themes are not susceptible of expression through a method of which it is the virtue to produce the idiosyncratic in the fine and strict sense of that word. Major themes, by definition of general and predominant interest, require for expression a method which produces the general in terms not of the idiosyncratic but the specific, and require, too, a form which seems to *contain* even more than to *imply* the wholeness beneath.

> In Lawrence you feel you have touched the plasm; in Miss Moore you feel you have escaped and come on the idea. The other life is there, but it is round the corner, not so much taken for granted as obliviated, not allowed to transpire, or if so only in the light ease of conversation: as we talk about famine in the Orient in discounting words that know all the time that it *might* be met face to face. In Miss Moore life is remote (life as good *and* evil) and everything is done to keep it remote; it is reality removed, but it is nonetheless reality, because we *know* that it is removed. This is perhaps another way of putting Kenneth Burke's hypothesis: "if she were discussing the newest model of automobile, I think she could somehow contrive to suggest an antiquarian's interest." Let us say that everything she gives is minutely precise, immediately accurate to the witnessing eye, but

that both the reality under her poems and the reality produced by them have a nostalgic quality, a hauntedness, that cannot be reached, and perhaps could not be borne, by these poems, if it were.

Yet . . . how could her poems be otherwise, or more? Her sensibility—the deeper it is the more persuaded it cannot give itself away—predicted her poetic method; and the defect of her method . . . only represents the idiosyncrasy of her sensibility: that it, like its subject matter, constitutes the perfection of standing aside.

2. "Masks of Ezra Pound":[10] Blackmur identified at least two fallacies in Pound. One he might have called the fallacy of surface articulation; the other, of unsupported anecdote (or allusion). There were other problems as well, and Blackmur did not hesitate to quote passages of the poetry to prove his point. Pound did his best work as a translator, he argued, time and again showing in his own original productions that he lacked the capacity to rise above a vivid articulation of commonplaces. Even poems like *Mauberley* and the better cantos were conventional, in the sense that they were actually translations or versions of other poems, or workings of material for which the relevant emotions were "agreed upon, or given, beforehand." The poems had—especially the Cantos—a semblance of unity, but had in fact no more than "the general sense of continuity . . . which may arise in the mind when read seriatim. The Cantos are what Mr. Pound himself called them in a passage now excised from the canon, a ragbag." One might admire the cadence, the phrasing, the subtle building-in of echoes in *Mauberley*, but one knew that the poem was "not complex," only "complicated," that to figure out a poem by Pound was to come to terms with the separate pieces and to register the ostensive ambition. One could not talk of ideas in the sense in which they came to life in Dante, Blake, or Yeats. There was in Pound no "reference to what is implicit and still to be said under the surface of what has already been said."

Blackmur's objection to the poet came down to his feeling that Pound was at best a master craftsman, a poet "supreme in the executive class," as he called him in the much shorter and later essay, "An Adjunct to the Muses'

10. In *Language as Gesture*, pp. 124–54.

Diadem."[11] Poets like Pound did refresh the language, quite as Pound earlier claimed he would, and he did set a good example for other poets who needed to be shown "what can be done with the instrument by skill and continuous practice." Supporters, like Eliot, who claimed for Pound something much greater, were wrong to see in his work a "criticism of life" such as we associate with Arnold and with Eliot himself. On the other hand, hostile critics like Yvor Winters pressed their opposition too hard, unable to accept Pound for the genuine felicities he managed. Pound knew less than Moore what his poetry could and could not accomplish, and he often supposed he was espousing a philosophy or offering a point of view when he was merely expressing irritation or putting together the stated positions of other men. He did know how to "set up" a verbal medium, as Blackmur noted, and to make the words sing within it; if we associate the achievement more with "a maker of great verse" than with "a great poet," we at least acknowledge that it was worth doing.

The passages selected to indicate Blackmur's case "against" Pound speak, really, for themselves, but it is important to note that the arguments are supported in the text by quotation from the poems. Also, for the thirty cantos Blackmur responded to, there is an extraordinary summary—about two pages in length—in which Blackmur demonstrates that it was not for failure to read Greek or inability to recognize allusions that he could not applaud Pound's performance.

> Mr. Pound's poetry has had from the beginning one constant character which qualifies deeply and subordinates to it every other character. It has been deliberately constructed as a series of surfaces or *personae;* it is a mask of Mr. Pound's best craftsmanship through which the voices of old times and our own are meant to be heard. Because the medium is verse, and private, the voices are an integral part of the mask, but whether because of choice or some radical limitation of talent, the voices are as a rule given indirectly, by allusive quotation or an alphabetical catalogue, and this is truer of Mr. Pound's original verse than of his translations. That is, the subject matter of his verse is, as it

11. Also in *Language as Gesture,* pp. 155–62.

were, behind the mask and apart from it in spite of the intention to the contrary, so that the reader is prevented from contact with the subject matter through the verse.

The success of Mr. Pound's mask depends on the critical labor performed, in which, before the success is apparent, the reader must share. The reader must know the original or enough of it to apprehend the surface Mr. Pound has made for it, exactly as the Roman audience had to know the substance of the myths they heard recounted through the actor's *personae.* For Mr. Pound's verse is not something new, substantially on its own feet, it is a surface set upon something already existing.

This deliberate disconnectedness, this art of a thing continually alluding to itself, continually breaking off short, is the method by which the Cantos tie themselves together . . . Success comes when the reader is forced by Mr. Pound's verbal skill to take the materials together; failure, when it occurs, is when Mr. Pound's words are not skillful enough and the internal dissensions are all that can be seen, or when the reader, as often, is simply ignorant of what is being talked about.

These effects, which may seem willful in the bad sense, are really necessary results of the anecdotal method as used by Mr. Pound. The presumption must always be, in an anecdote, that the subject and its import are known before the story is begun; they cannot be given in the anecdote itself. An anecdote illustrates, it does not present its subject; its purpose is always ulterior or secondary.

3. "Notes on E. E. Cummings' Language":[12] When Helen Vendler, in her own recent piece on Cummings, described Blackmur's argument as "unanswerable," she meant obviously that the argument had been made as thoroughly and as carefully as anyone could wish. One might dispute the verdict, but one would then be required to dispute as well the terms of the argument. One might, for example, contend that vagueness is a positive attribute in a certain kind of poetry, and that Cummings chose to write poems at once jaunty and sentimental because he was reacting against practices that had influenced American poetry too long. Blackmur notes that Cummings was part of "the anti-culture group; what has been called at various times vorticism, futurism, dadaism, surrealism, and so on." Which is

12. In *Language as Gesture,* pp. 317–40.

to say, he thought he was doing his best by going against the grain of the literary values espoused by the academy and by the high-toned Reviews of his day. The critic objects to "a sentimental denial of the intelligence" in Cummings, though defenders have easy recourse to the view "that the unintelligible is the only object of significant experience." Blackmur knew the game. He would probably have agreed with Vendler, looking back on his essay, that the argument was unanswerable but knew better than to expect that most others would wish to conduct their inquiries with his standards in hand.

What makes the Cummings essay—more than any other Blackmur wrote—*seem* unanswerable, is its relentless zeroing in on a single "fallacy." Cummings's practice is described as taking several different directions, but all seem to come out of a habit of thought that impresses itself in all the poems in the same way. Blackmur grants to the poet sincerity of motive and even a certain excellence of invention, whatever that can be worth in the context of such an essay. He denies him, though, any possibility of genuine achievement. Cummings's method, reflecting as it does his insupportable and stubborn habit of mind, will not allow achievement. Take up any poem by the man, Blackmur says, moving from book to book, lifting out here a line or an image, there another and another: wherever you look you will find a stultifying sameness, a limp formula parading as novelty or bluntness. In no other essay does Blackmur isolate so many single words and images and hold them up to analysis and rebuke. The reader of the essay may continue to feel an affection for Cummings, but he will not wish to return to the poems before putting Blackmur's analysis well out of mind. Such a reader will not be, in Blackmur's terms, a reader at all, for he will come to poetry only to have his own vague sentiments confirmed or flattered. Blackmur's fatal dissection of Cummings will seem to that reader not unanswerable but a typical instance of critical meddling, the rational intelligence trying to interfere with the exercise of "free and instructed intuition." Blackmur knew his man, and knew his loyal readers too.

Any one of a dozen paragraphs in the essay may be used to exhibit the case Blackmur made against Cummings, but I want to single out two passages: one, for a statement of the fallacy, the other for a modest demonstration of the poet-critic at words. It is a fitting way to end this essay. And Blackmur, of course, speaks best when he speaks for himself.

> Now it is evident that this word [flower] must attract Mr. Cummings' mind very much; it must contain for him an almost unlimited variety and extent of meaning . . . The question is, whether or not the reader can possibly have shared the experience which Mr. Cummings has had of the word . . . "Flower," like every other word not specifically the expression of a logical relation, began life as a metaphor, as a leap from feeling to feeling, as a bridge in the imagination to give meaning to both those feelings. Presumably, the amount of meaning possible to the word is increased with each use, but only the meaning *possible*. Actually, in practice, a very different process goes on. Since people are occupied mostly with communication and argument and conversation . . . words are commonly spoken and written with the *least* possible meaning preserved, instead of the most. History is taken for granted, ignored, or denied. Only the outsides of words, so to speak, are used; and doubtless the outsides of words are all that the discursive intellect needs. But when a word is used in a poem it should be the sum of all its appropriate history made concrete and particular in the individual context; and in poetry all words act *as if* they were so used, because the only kind of meaning poetry can have requires that all its words resume their full life: the full life being modified and made unique by the qualifications the words perform one upon the other in the poem . . . An author should remember . . . that the reality of a word is anterior to, and greater than, his use of it can ever be; that there is a perfection to the feelings in words to which his mind cannot hope to attain, but that his chief labor will be toward the approximation of that perfection.

Mr. Cummings has a fine talent for using familiar, even almost dead words, in such a context as to make them suddenly impervious to every ordinary sense; they become unable to speak, but with a great air of being bursting with something very important and precise to say. "The bigness of cannon is *skillful* . . . enormous rhythm of *absurdity* . . . *slimness* of *evenslicing* eyes are chisels . . . electric Distinct face haughtily vital *clinched* in a swoon of *synopsis* . . . my friend's being continually whittles *keen* careful futile *flowers*," etc. With the possible exception of the compound *evenslicing* the italicized words are all ordinary words; all in normal contexts have a variety of meanings both connotative and denotative; the particular context being such as to indicate a particular meaning.

Mr. Cummings' contexts are employed to an opposite purpose in so far as they wipe out altogether the history of the word, its past associations and general character . . . Something precise is no doubt intended; the warrant for the belief is in the almost violent isolation into which the words are thrown; but that precision can seldom, by this method, become any more than just that "something precise." The reality, the event, the feeling, which we will allow Mr. Cummings has in mind, is not sensibly in the word. It is one thing for meaning to be difficult, or abstruse—hidden in its heart, that is. "Absent thee from *felicity* a while," Blake's "Time is the *mercy* of eternity" are reasonable examples; there the mystery is inside the words. In Mr. Cummings' words the mystery flies in the face, is on the surface; because there is no inside, no realm of possibility, of essence.